My Favorite Mother-In-Law

Table of contents

My Favorite Mother-In-Law

This book is memoir. It reflects the author's present recollections of experiences over time. Some names, characteristics, and locations have been changed, some events have been compressed, and some dialogue has been recreated.

Aging

I've been twenty-five for about four decades. This month, I awoke to find I'm suddenly sixty-five. I use adverbs sparingly, but in this case, "suddenly" fits.

Sixty-five is harder than twenty-five.

When I was twenty-five, I could run a five-minute mile. I flipped a canoe on my shoulders, then down, then up again sixteen times in thirty seconds. I could carry a 250 pound load up a sand dune.

Now my back hurts when I get out of bed in the morning.

When I was twenty-five, I played bass guitar in a rock-and-roll band. I learned music theory. I picked up the banjo and taught myself to sight-read.

Now I can't remember where I put my keys, much less the key signature of the music I'm practicing.

To document my *sudden* aging, the United States government sends me paperwork about Social Security and Medicare. I laugh about how those are for old people. I stop laughing when I realize I'm the old people they are talking about.

I have grandchildren. My hair and beard are white. My skin is thinner, my knees complain when I stand up. Industry head-hunters have stopped calling me with job offers.

When I was twenty-five, I strove to be respected by my peers. I worked hard for a fine patina of wisdom. Now I find that patina is easy to come by; it's called "liver spots."

This is the first time I've gotten old and I am totally unprepared. I was hoping the literature accompanying the Medicare paperwork would offer a seminar (hopefully in some exotic location) about aging gracefully. There are such seminars, but they are taught by forty-year-old celebrities and are mainly concerned about choosing make-up and fashion. Nothing about how an old white guy is supposed to proceed with confidence. (Of course, old white men have never lacked for an undeserved sense of confidence.)

I realize I should observe someone older than myself. If I paid careful attention, I could see their triumphs and their failures. I could take careful notes and optimize my own experience. I need a mentor to show me how to get older.

Fortunate me: I have a perfect mentor.

My favorite Mother-In-Law!

Greta

I've only been married once, so Greta is my *only* mother-in-law. It amuses me to tell her this. Greta always laughs and give me a hug. She calls me "Marky."

I've known Greta for forty years and she likes to tell me stories about growing up. When we are hanging out together, I'll fix her a Wisconsin Old Fashioned (Brandy and 7-up with an orange slice and a bright-red maraschino cherry) and ask her questions. She'll repeat stories she has told me before, but then I ask her deeper questions.

"Oh, you are really picking my brain now," she says. She looks into the forty years before we met, then comes back. I know that's a sign I'm going to hear something new and always unexpected.

Greta was born in 1934 outside of Dorchester, Wisconsin. Her father maintained a small dairy herd and opened a roadside tavern where she helped serve roasted chicken and beer. Her dad served minors, although he was quick to tell these kids "you've had enough" and made it clear drinking was not an opportunity to harass his daughters.

She loved her dad; he would take her to town when he went for business and buy her a treat. Her sister was jealous, and Greta told her that Dad would take her as well—she just needed to ask. Apparently she never did.

She saw friends deal with date rape and unwanted pregnancies. She knows pregnancies don't always go well. Greta lived through the polio epidemic. To her, vaccines are a miracle.

Greta went to college to become a teacher. She has told us (several times) about her experience in teachers college. She was in charge of the finances for at least one of the annual trips and we have seen the pictures, diary entries, and budget. Greta was quite the spark plug, singing and dancing until early in the morning, then getting her fellow students up and in the buses for another day driving through the mountains.

Greta first met Gene Ross at the dance hall in Dorchester, Wisconsin in 1951. They kept in touch while Gene was stationed in the Chorwan Valley of Korea. I'm not privileged enough to have read any of their letters, but I have seen the newspaper clippings and service papers saved by Gene's mother. I only knew Gene as a quiet and steady man; it's difficult to imagine him firing a 105 mm howitzer or placing 24 M16 rockets into a T66 launcher. He returned after fifteen months and never talked about the shrapnel in his arm.

Greta married Gene in 1956. She birthed five children in Neillsville, Wisconsin. In 1950, the population was 2,663 people. In 2020 the population was at 2,384. Not much has changed in seventy years.

Greta carried a hand-packed lunch down to Gene at his Citgo service station and did the banking for the business. They purchased a four-bedroom, two bath house with 1,800 square feet of floor space for a rambunctious family. Upstairs were two bedrooms; boys on the left, girls on the right. Gene and Greta had a bedroom downstairs, the fourth bedroom was Gene's office.

Her children, like all children, tested her limits. Her youngest son memorized joke books and would repeat them, rapid-fire, at the dinner table. By the time the kids were laughing, choking, and spitting up milk from their noses, Gene sent them to the basement. I picture Gene and Greta sitting at the quiet table, trying to keep an air of somber wisdom, but eventually smirking and breaking out in snorts themselves.

One daughter was famous for sneaking out from her second-floor bedroom by climbing down the antenna mast next to the house. She had to avoid the nearby kitchen window, especially if anyone was doing late night dishes. Once, upon her return, she was halfway up the mast when a passing car caught her in its headlights. I'm told the car stopped for a minute, then drove on. She continued her climb and nothing more was ever said. That word never travelled back to Gene and Greta is surprising considering a town the size of Neillsville.

One son collected beer cans. A *lot* of beer cans; empty ones. *Who emptied all those beer cans?*

This family of seven traveled extensively: Ohio, Michigan, South Dakota, Florida, the Spokane World Fair, Idaho, Colorado, the Apostle Islands in Lake Superior, New York City, Colorado and more. The chariot was a 1971 Ford Country Squire with wood-like side panels. Enough room for everyone, but I've heard there were fights anyways.

Janell tells me she ignored several of the scenic overlooks in favor of reading steamy stories in the back of *RedBook* magazine and learning how to kiss boys. In contrast, I was reading *Boy's Life,* learning how to start fires and run away from bears. This explains a lot about the early years of our marriage.

Greta has no trust issues

Greta and I conversed over the phone a year before I met her in person. I had returned from a trip and wanted to follow up on a potential romance with Janell Ross, but didn't have her phone number. This was before the internet, so I went to a phone booth and called directory assistance—411 for those who don't remember the number.

"Directory assistance," said the operator. This was a real person—not a recording, not an AI. "What city are you calling?"

"Um, Neillsville, Wisconsin?" I had a letter with a return address of Neillsville, so I assumed I could reach her there. "I'm looking for Janell Ross."

"I don't have a Janell Ross. I do have a Eugene Ross. I can connect you with that number."

"That works." The phone clicked and rang. A voice answered.

"This is Greta," said the voice on the phone.

"Hi Greta," I replied. "I don't think you know me, but I'm trying to call Janell. Can I get her phone number?"

Greta didn't ask me if I was a stalker, or suggest I could give her *my* phone number and she would pass it to Janell, or anything related to protecting her daughter from miscreants. She didn't pause before giving me

Janell's phone number in Green Bay, Wisconsin. It didn't occur to me she should be a bit less trusting than she was.

That's Greta.

Meeting Greta

I first met Greta when I was twenty-four years old. Janell, who is now my favorite wife, introduced me to her family. I was too self-confident to be nervous about how they might feel about me. As long as I didn't smoke pot in the living room after dinner, I would get high marks.

I knew nothing about Neillsville until I went there with Janell. We drove into town and I started laughing.

"What's so funny?" asked Janell.

"Ely is bigger than this. We're in the sticks," I replied. Ely, Minnesota is a small town on the border of the Boundary Waters Canoe Area; I spent my summers as a canoe guide at a camp nearby. When I wasn't goofing around in the north woods, I lived in St. Paul, Minnesota and had a decidedly superior attitude about the sophistication of cities as a function of their population.

"Neillsville is where I grew up," Janell informed me. Her tone was frosty. I decided it was best to keep my thoughts on sophistication vs population to myself. It was not a topic to pursue if I was hoping to get lucky.

We entered town on Highway 10 through downtown, took a left at highway 73, drove through a dying downtown and crossed O'Neill Creek. From there, it's a short drive to the family home and double-car garage. We pulled up in the driveway and honked.

I stand about Six-Foot, Two-Inches tall; the tallest of all the Niemann kids. My dad had the nickname of "shorty," which I originally thought was because of his height, but later learned it was due to his haircut. I am genetically like my grandfather, Louie, who stood 6-foot-6 and towered over Ella, his five-foot-and-a-little-bit-short wife.

Greta is about five-foot-nothing and barely comes up to my armpit. When I first met Greta, she came out to the front door as I was unfolding myself from the front seat of my surplus postal jeep. She gave me an unflinching hug in spite of the road odor I carried. To return her hug I had to bend over-almost getting down on my knees to equalize our height. She was so damned pleased to meet me.

Janell and I married, had kids, moved from the Midwest to Wyoming, then Colorado, then Portland, Oregon. Gene died shortly after we moved into our Portland home. Greta kept showing up. We have a spare bedroom and she loves to clean house. I told her several times she should move to Portland. She laughed and turned us down each time. I wasn't kidding.

Greta and I had one particular conversation I remember. We were walking on the Oregon coast, just the two of us. We got to talking about abortion and her Catholic faith. I'm a liberal Presbyterian, but she never held that against me. I was explaining my stance on abortion, expressing my belief abortion was a medical issue and was a decision between a woman and her doctor. The church she belongs to was unwavering in the belief that abortion was wrong. Nevertheless, we had an open and respectful discussion about the issue, she gracefully accepted my thoughts, which gave me encouragement to accept hers.

Religion

Janell grew up Catholic. We married at my childhood church, North Como Presbyterian in Roseville, Minnesota. To cover all of our theological bases, we enlisted a Presbyterian minister and a Catholic Deacon to officiate.

In response to the wedding announcement, we received a letter from Janell's aunt, who shared her disappointment that Janell was marrying outside the Catholic religion. I suppose she expected I would convert to Catholicism.

The Catholic church, for their part, refused to allow me to participate in Catholic sacraments since I was a protestant outcast. My emotions have mellowed over the years, but I still clench my teeth when I recall the conversation with the Catholic Father at a premarriage encounter I attended with Janell. The Priest informed me I was *persona non grata* and would have to remain seated during the celebration of mass. The internet provides pages of rationalization about why this is, but none of it dampens the sting of segregation.

But then, there's Greta. She never brought this up. Never. Not once. She loved me for who I was. She overlooked my faith, my bad hygiene, my goofy dress code. She only saw the man her daughter loved and the potential I had as a son-in-law.

She loves her gay nephew. She's seen men (and priests) misbehave and small town voices hush it up. Greta will tell you we are God's children and we are less than perfect, but we still deserve God's love. Who are we to judge?

Fun-gi

Greta laughs at my jokes. When we visit she looks past Janell to see if I'm there. If I am, Janell is dismissed and I get the first hug. I've told Greta she is my favorite mother-in-law (she is my *only* mother-in-law) and she agrees that I am her favorite son-in-law. (The other son-in-law is aware of this but chooses to ignore my little insults).

My role in Greta's life is comedic relief—I'm the fun guy. With apologies to the family members who wrangle medications and bills and doctor visits, my job is to make Greta laugh. When Greta is feeling blue, I put on my walking shoes, leave my home in Portland, Oregon, and drive five days to Stevens Point, Wisconsin. I stay for a week, usually longer.

I'm not sure why I have a close relationship with Greta. We didn't survive a plane crash in the Alps, foraging for food together in the frozen mountains. She didn't donate one of her kidneys to save me from a terminal illness. I've never borrowed money from her. Perhaps once for ice cream. But still, when I see her, my heart sings.

I'm sad our time together is drawing to a close.

Kitchen

Greta and her kitchen were legendary. Everyone was fed and watered from the moment they arrived until the last hand of Sheepshead was played. Even then, she would pack a sandwich for the trip home. Greta called it "a little lunch."

When I recall my early memories of Greta, she is always in *her kitchen*. I emphasize "her kitchen" on purpose. I recall being able to sit at the table; I don't recall standing and talking. I would have been in the way.

I wrote an article for *Wired* magazine about Greta. The Apple Macintosh had just been introduced and the software industry was realizing command-line interfaces were ugly and non-intuitive. We started to use phrases like "user-friendly", "point-and-click" and "windows." I experienced Greta waltzing around her kitchen, manipulating the oven and stove like a set of precision jeweler's tools. My story reflected on the relationship between Greta and her range, imploring my peers to aspire to the same relationship between these new computers and the people that would use them.

The stove was avocado green with a glass-top range, an electric oven and a warmer drawer. There was a clock with hands (not digital) and if you read the instructions, you could use the timer to turn the oven on and off. When Greta was in motion, the kitchen smelled of frying pork chops and onions.

For thirty years, she cooked three meals a day without fail and without complaint. I wasn't there to observe Janell's formative years, but I can only imagine the uproar of slinging breakfast for five children, some late for school, some needing a diaper change. Gene did what he could, ate a half piece of toast, washed it down with a cup of coffee and went to the gas station.

I have first-hand experience of what Greta considered an acceptable dinner. It wasn't fancy, but it was plentiful and satisfying. It was delivered to the table with the timing of a professional chef. It was warm. The family prayed, and Greta always added how she was lucky to have such a good provider. I remember thinking that if I was to continue this relationship with Janell, there were pretty clear expectations of my role in any resulting marriage.

"Eat it, then it will be gone," Greta would say, passing the entree and salad around the table a third time. The refrigerator was full of leftovers from yesterday until she brought out plates for snacking on during the evening family game.

It's important to understand how competently Greta managed her family. For many years, I participated in software trade shows. These were enormously over-blown events, monuments to the egos of the company presidents, pundits, and companies pushing the latest and greatest. A trade show was a nightmare of logistics and last-minute stress-inducing capriciousness. One company president decided the color of the booth was all wrong and forced his employees to repaint the evening before the show. This is just about the equivalent of deciding to remodel the kitchen the evening before a Thanksgiving dinner. Complete madness. It brought people to tears. I'm not kidding.

Greta would have handled it. The booth would have been painted. And pinstriped. And she would have fixed lunch for the out-of-his-mind CEO who suggested a repaint in the first place. Then she would have headed back home to prepare dinner for her family.

Fire

Greta lived alone after Gene died. She moved to a new house a few blocks away. We noticed she was willing to let us cook. Over time, she *expected* we would cook meals. Slowly, we picked up clues her interest in the kitchen was waning. For anyone else, this might be just a symptom of living alone. But this was unsettling for those of us who knew Greta.

"The neighbor's house burned down yesterday," she told Janell over the phone. "It was over on the next block."

"Oh no," Janell said. "What did you do?"

"Oh, nothing," Greta replied. "I could see it burning and I thought someone should call the fire department."

"Mom, *you* should have called the fire department!"

"I suppose. How are you doing in school?"

Greta was losing interest in her kitchen and her neighborhood. The siblings realized it was time to move Greta out of her home and into someplace with more resources; a nice apartment in the independent wing of Evergreen Meadows Senior Community in Stevens Point, Wisconsin. We have a video of Greta sticking out her tongue at us as she unhappily left her home in Neillsville.

Sundowning

My experience with Greta has always been delightful. Not just positive, I truly enjoy her presence. She makes me laugh, is never judgmental, exhibits all the best features of her Christian faith. So Greta's evil twin was unexpected. We met her after we left the wedding of one of the grandsons.

It had been a long and festive event, attended by the entire Ross clan. There are more of them than there are of me. They all know who I am and they take perverse delight in asking trivia questions about their family history. I should have commissioned flash cards and had Janell drill me on names, birthdays, city of residence, five pertinent facts of each uncle and aunt. At the least I should have practiced drawing the Ross family tree on a large sheet of poster board.

I have a cousin who excels at this game of *Do You Remember?* He will tell you about the party you were at when someone dropped a cake on the picnic table. I will have no recollection of the picnic, nor being at the picnic, nor dropping the cake. At this point, he could tell me any outlandish lie and I would believe it.

But...the grandson's wedding. It was a massive Ross reunion (as are they all) and I was exhausted. I suspect Janell and Greta were as well. We had rented a hotel room nearby, planned to get some sleep, then drive home the following day. We drove off, leaving the kids to the dance floor and wedding hi-jinks. Greta was in the back seat, Janell and I in front.

"I cannot believe I have such ungrateful children," Greta suddenly speaks up in the dark. "I am going to give all of my money to charity and you will get none of it."

This was *not* spoken in a teasing voice. Greta was serious and angry. Greta's norm is happy and tolerant, loving and expansive. This was Evil Greta. Who the hell is in the back seat and how am I supposed to react? Know that I am conflict-avoidant and this was already one large conflict. I was happy to be driving and decided to focus on avoiding deer jumping from the forest.

There *had* been an incident at the wedding. One of Greta's children felt it was appropriate to proselytize to one of the grandchildren and his girlfriend. His words were unwelcome and caused tears, leaving the rest of us to mitigate this emotional exchange. Greta may have heard some of the discussion. That's what I assumed this was about. But Greta wouldn't say what was bothering her, only that she was disgusted with us.

Janell and I didn't understand what was happening. Looking back, there were clues, but we didn't know to look for them. At the hotel, she wanted me to get her suitcase out of the car; I had seen her place it in the closet just five minutes before. She asked twice why we were staying in this strange room.

She was angry and sullen until the following morning when we joined some of the grandkids for breakfast. Over waffles, bacon, and coffee she perked up and we were again in good graces. Evil Greta was gone.

In the next months and years, Evil Greta periodically reappeared. We would receive nasty emails and phone calls. The next morning she would be chipper and friendly. She had no recollection of sending us an email with ALL CAPS ABOUT THE LATEST EVILS IN THE MODERN WORLD!!!!!

It didn't help that she was surrounded by angry voices on the television and neighborhood, convinced the world was coming unglued and Satan was in the White House. She received a daily stream of hate-filled emails, alarming news reports, sanctimonious religious pamphlets. Some of these she forwarded to her children. It was not what I would have expected from the gentle Greta who accepted me for who I was.

When my son was thirteen, he sprayed me with the garden hose. He thought it was funny. I was pissed, and let him know by subjecting him to my traditional family silent treatment. In a brief time, I realized I had broken his spirit and he was feeling bad about himself. I gave him a hug, but realized I had damaged the relationship; there would never be a way to undo the hurt. So it was with Greta—the gentle woman who had given me her daughter's phone number was no longer the same.

In time, we learned this is called *sundowning*. It is an early indicator of dementia, often associated with Alzheimer's disease. It's a real thing, there's research being done. When it happens it is distressing and scary. Janell and I have learned to distract her away from whatever is causing her to be upset. Sometimes I sing a song with her or tell her a joke. I wish I had the joke book her son had memorized for dinner times.

Over a short period of time, Greta became confused with how to operate email and the nastygrams ceased. But this new Greta was living with all of us.

The Independent Life

Life in the independent wing of Evergreen Meadows Senior Community is akin to a college dorm: without the heavy drinking, overactive sexuality, and loud rock music. Maybe it is—I don't have surveillance camera footage to confirm my assumptions. I do know the male/female ratio is in favor of the men.

Greta's apartment has a kitchen and her kitchen has the equipment from her previous home. She has the capacity to prepare a meal for thirty relatives, plus sending them home with a bag of sandwiches for the ride home. Seating might be a challenge, she has a total of six chairs.

The unfortunate hair in the lasagna is that Greta has moved in during the Covid pandemic. Evergreen Meadows Senior Community is on lock-down. Nobody is allowed to share their viruses and kill their fellow residents. A good call, but a damper on Greta's ability to form friendships with her new community.

But, as Dr. Ian Malcolm dryly observes, "Life finds a way." (Jurassic Park. Look it up.) Evergreen Meadows Senior Community simply doesn't have enough staff to police the halls all day and all night.

Greta's new friend Bobbi shows up at the door, knocks, and Greta lets her in. Virus be damned.

"Want to have a beer?" Bobbi asks.

"Are we allowed to drink beer here?" Greta asks.

"I don't know," admits Bobbi. "Let's grab one and sneak into the hall closet."

I am not making this up. The Evergreen Meadows Senior Community marketing director will attest to the fact of finding Greta and Bobbi in the staircase, drinking a clandestine beer. She asked them why they were sneaking around and got the full story. By the way, independent residents can do anything they damn well please, as long as it doesn't scare the staff. Drinking beer in the staircase, or their room, or the common spaces is allowed. But it's much more fun if it's not.

Changes

Greta is losing her sense of time as a linear experience. As she ages, her brain no longer files events in chronological sequence. Events in the past are classified as dreams, rather than "something I did yesterday afternoon." She knows this is happening, and it frightens her.

I understand. My father was an engineer. He worked on the space shuttle, built his own house and dreamed up a way to compete at crossword puzzles. He rarely lost.

As he aged, he noticed his diminished ability to remember specifics. He stopped working on crossword puzzles. He was fearful one day he wouldn't grasp the concept of a matrix.

Greta is facing a transition.

Independent. Assisted. Memory.

There is a standard progression of events in a senior living facility. First is independent living: a standard apartment. Independent living comes with housekeeping, maintenance, a meal plan, free bus transportation, and a watchful staff. It's a bit pricey, but only if you don't consider the value of a full support staff.

Next is assisted living. It looks much the same as independent, but includes enhanced staff involvement. When you don't remember to take your pills or show up for meals, assisted living is there to help. Independent living means you can sit alone in your room if you wish. But isolation is bad for both body and mind. Assisted living means there is a nice lady down the hall checking in on you to make sure you're okay. It just happens the nice lady is part of the staff and has an emergency call button and a nursing degree.

Later we'll talk about the memory care wing. But it's not time for that yet.

Transition to Assisted Living

The Evergreen Meadows Senior Community kitchen staff are efficient and precise. There's a lot of food to prepare and it needs to be served warm, arriving at the table in a narrow window of time. Their budget precludes juggling a fluid schedule of reservations. Show up according to the plan, please, or miss dinner.

Greta wasn't making it to breakfast, lunch, or dinner. In the past, when she controlled the meal schedule, things happened with a careful eye to the clock. Gene finished work at 6:00 pm, drove home in five minutes, washed his hands and sat down at the table. Dinner was on the table at 6:08 pm every evening. Given her history of running *her kitchen* in the way she saw fit, I'm not surprised she pushed back on being told when to show up for meals.

Nobody is going to tell Greta when dinner is served. She may be small, but she is mighty, and dinner will be ready when she says it's ready. *Understand?*

Greta wasn't eating. She didn't venture out of her room. She called her children, telling them she was alone and afraid and hungry. She wanted to return to her home where she knew where the kitchen was and where her friends were and where she could walk to St. Mary's Catholic Church.

She didn't say it directly, but she needed assistance. So her children accommodated her needs. Greta made her first move at Evergreen Meadows Senior Community, leaving her apartment in the independent wing for a smaller room in the assisted portion of the building. The staff began looking in to suggest she go for a meal, or Mass, or bingo. They couldn't tell her what to do, but they were aggressively helpful.

She regained weight. She made friends and was invited to sit at table number one (an honor). Her world expanded. She was more talkative and friendly.

The Fall

Greta is nimble. She can stand on one leg to put on her pants. I do yoga so I can emulate her. So far, I'm about fifty-percent crashing into the wall and alarming the household with my feeble attempt at dressing myself. I try not to embarrass myself, but frequently fail.

Greta proceeds through her life with the grace of a ballerina. Maybe I exaggerate; she doesn't have a barre or wall mirror in her apartment. But I dare you to challenge her to a balance contest. She's unnatural that way.

Imagine our surprise when she winds up in the emergency room due to a fall. Nobody knows what happened for sure, but she was probably trying to wash her feet in the sink. One foot to support herself, one foot in the sink. Try it yourself; I'll advise you to put a mattress on the floor to catch you *when* you fall.

Maybe she was performing gymnastic floor exercises. Maybe she was swinging from the light fixtures. Maybe she was working on her *arabesque* in preparation for the upcoming talent show.

Nobody knows what happened, but we got a call from the hospital. There were no broken bones, but other things were not good. Her systems were failing. She had infections. She was sundowning—*hard*. She referred to the nurses as *devil's spawn*. She was not a pleasant patient.

The hospital checked her fluids and undercarriage, but there was nothing wrong outside of dehydration and old age. Insurance insisted the hospital discharge her. She wasn't sick enough to stay, but she was sick enough to qualify for hospice care. Greta was going to die.

Greta needed all hands on deck twenty-four hours of care, seven days a week. Get her to drink water. Get her up and out of bed. Work on her mobility. Improve her state of mind.

Here's the catch. If you need 24x7 care, you can't move back to Evergreen Meadows Senior Community. They don't have the license or personnel required to provide that level of support. But you can't remain housed at the hospital, insurance only pays for a limited time. Her only option was a rehab facility, cold and sterile and designed to make patients want to get better and get out. Greta would have to find a new place to live out her days and her options were few.

Here's the loophole. *If the siblings hired 24x7 care for Greta then she could return to Evergreen Meadows*. But damn, that's expensive!

There are a few details I haven't mentioned just yet:

Janell retired a few months previous.

Janell has a medical degree.

I have a job which doesn't require I be in any particular place at any time.

What to do?

The Siblings

Greta and Gene raised five children: three girls, two boys. There were more conceived, but these ended in miscarriages. Gene and Greta picked up the pieces and moved on.

I'm told I had an additional older sister besides the two I grew up with. There were complications, and a doctor told my parents they were done having children. In spite of what he told them, I'm here. I'd like to meet this doctor and review his methodology, general knowledge, and conclusions.

Janell and I have two children, both of whom were enthusiastically welcomed. At one point in our early lives, we were traveling for several months. Janell's period was late, so we went to a Seattle planned parenthood for a pregnancy test. Apparently this was before the day of a drugstore pee-on-a-stick.

Janell provided whatever fluids the clinic requested, then we sat in the waiting room. Strangely, I don't remember discussing the impact a pregnancy would have on our trip, much less our lives.

"Janell, you can come in now," the nurse said. "First door on your right."

We walked in, closed the door, sat down. Again, I can't remember our conversation while we waited. But I do remember the excitement. When we travel, we deal with the unexpected and find the enjoyment of the moment. This was another unexpected event; we would find the enjoyable path through.

There was a small knock at the door and a woman in a lab coat enters, accompanied by the nurse. She has a piece of paper. This part of my memory plays out like a reality show reveal, where there is a dramatic statement ("And this week's star baker is…") followed by reaction shots of several faces, followed by the verdict ("… MARSHA!")

“Well, Janell,” the white coat says, “you’re....”

[insert dramatic reaction shots; Janell. Mark. The nurse. Everyone in the waiting room. The fictional film crew.]

“...not pregnant!”

Janell and I express disappointment. We were ready for an adventure. We were ready for a pregnancy. Not today.

“That’s not the usual reaction,” says the white coat. “Most people are relieved or happy to hear this. I guess, well, I’m sorry?”

We held hands and walked out the door. I’m not sure we told our travel friends.

Janell and I have never experienced a miscarriage in our personal lives. Janell, as a midwife, has experienced many, as well as the heartbreak of fetal demise. I’m part of Janell’s support network, so I vicariously experience her grief.

I believe Greta loves her five children with the extra capacity of those two miscarriages. Gene was a quiet man, but I know he did as well. I saw him demonstrate this love in quiet ways.

Janell brought me home to meet her parents one holiday. At the end of the visit, we loaded up the Buick Skylark (Engine: V6; one hundred and fifty-five horsepower; paint: blue; rust: yes; mpg: [see *Engine* above]) and drove to the gas station to say goodbye to Gene. We drove over the bell cable (*ding ding*) and Gene came out. He filled the gas tank, checked the oil, forgot to charge us, said goodbye. When I got back in the car I could see he was holding back tears. I don’t think that was part of the everyday service he offered to other customers.

Greta’s children have dispersed themselves across the United States. The oldest son one lives eight miles from Evergreen Meadows Senior Community; Janell lives 1,944. Siblings number three, four, and five are respectively overseas, sixty-seven miles, and 1,055 miles. Likewise, the siblings are at different points in their careers; the younger they are, the less flexible their job. Personal visits become more difficult as distance increases or a career demands.

They love her in their unique ways. One son fiercely protects her religion. One daughter shows her pictures. Another son sings her songs. Another daughter fixes her hair. All visit and call on a regular basis.

But providing twenty-four/seven rehabilitation care is a big ask. Professional rehab nurses are difficult to find and expensive, and for a good reason. It's unrealistic to ask anyone to give up family, life, and career.

Janell and I decided to take on the job. Our lives are flexible and we have the freedom to relocate at whim.

Greta needing care was just another unexpected event; we would find the enjoyable path through.

How I Got Here

For two months, I have been the youngest resident of my mother-in-law's senior community. I am a mere sixty-five-years old and am told I'm an interloper, an outsider to this community with no hope of truly joining for another fifteen years.

In contrast to my older friends at Evergreen Meadows Senior Community, my knees still work, I do yoga balance poses without a chair, and I (occasionally) win at pickleball. I eat and drink pretty much what I like and I stay up past 9:00 p.m. All of these disqualify me from living at Evergreen Meadows Senior Community.

Yet, here I am. How did that happen?

Housing

The God I worship doth not smite nor crush nor strike down mine enemies. But oh, man—watch out for that omnipotent sense of humor. I'm certain God has a dashboard next to his almighty throne. The dashboard is covered with an infinite number of push-buttons. Each button has the name of one of his children.

When he deems it necessary, he speaks in a booming voice, saying "I have called you by name, you are mine." With a flourish big enough to encompass a universe, he pushes a button. One of the angels working in Heavenly IT Support notes a display, flashing the words "Custard Cream Pie Successfully Delivered." Here on Earth, these metaphorical pies-in-the-face manifest themselves in many ways. For some, it is a slip on a banana peel. For others, being chased by a rooster through a cow pasture.

God turns to St. Peter with a smile and says, "Wouldst thou likest to wager upon Mark? Five drachma sayeth he will accepteth any crazy idea I sendeth to his path."

With a sigh, St. Peter puts down his clipboard outlining the days agenda. It's difficult to keep an omnipresent deity focused on one task. "I accepth." He shrugs. It's the only way to get God back on track.

God pushes my button, a custard pie is delivered and manifests as a lack of housing in Stevens Point.

My Custard Cream Pie

When we first arrive in Stevens Point, Janell and I try to stay in Greta's room. Evergreen Meadows Senior Community frowns upon this co-habitation. For our part, we chafe at the closeness of three of us 24 by 7, side by side. I imagine it's as claustrophobic as riding in a 1971 Ford Country Squire from Wisconsin to Florida, but without seat belts.

I investigate long-term residency at the neighboring Holiday Inn: $3,000 per month. No free breakfast, but access to the pool, weight room, and as many towels as you want. That's a lot of moola for sleeping next to the Clark County Fireman's Convention—or the FFA Regional Expo. Both events are loud and rowdy. Also not a solution.

I investigate AirBnB. There are no month-long stays available. I can string several one-week stays end-to-end, living the life of an urban nomad. We'll spend more time moving than making Greta laugh. This, too: not a solution.

We can purchase a house. We can then furnish the house. We can start service for electric, water, sewer, and garbage. Or we can hang out with Greta—but not both. Obviously not a solution.

We can rent an apartment—for a minimum of six months. Or not, because Stevens Point has no available six month leases. This is also not a solution.

The Solution

Janell and I sit in the lobby discussing our predicament when Jenna, the Director of Marketing for Evergreen Meadows Senior Community, joins us.

"I think I have something you'd be interested in hearing," Jenna says.

Janell and I perk up. Jenna is a source of local information with all the important contacts a Director of Marketing needs. She's friendly and we talk with her often. Maybe she's found a spare loft in the warehouse district. Maybe it has a floor and walls. Maybe it has vermin, but those I can deal with.

"We have a spare two-bedroom unit in the independent wing," she tells us. "It's not furnished, but comes with a meal plan. We can give it to you on a limited basis for the price of a single."

This means we would be within a two-minute walk of Greta's front door. And did I mention this is happening during a Wisconsin winter? Any way to avoid going outside is a bonus.

Janell and I realize this is our best (*only*) solution. We sign and are now residents of Evergreen Meadows Senior Community.

In heaven, Saint Peter loses the bet (again). He curses and hands God a fiver. Betting with an all-knowing being is a losing proposition.

Room 202

This room is quiet, but not lonely.

To the east are sunny windows shining a pattern of light on a red chair. Miles Davis shares his genius of vibrating the air I breathe. Outside and one floor below me is a sidewalk where Tom and Pauline are walking Zero, their Norwich Terrier. Foxes (the furry kind with tails) live in the vacant lot to the southwest of the apartments next door. I've made coffee; I can get kitchen coffee from downstairs but mine is way stronger than they are willing to brew.

Janell is downstairs with Greta. They are participating in *Drum Fit*, an exercise class requiring a chair, drum sticks, and a stability ball. Jenny (from a video screen) calls out rhythms and demonstrates suggested application of sticks to ball. She's a blonde Taiko drummer, infusing her energy into the room filled with senior citizens of limited mobility and stability.

I'll join them at 11:30 am for lunch in the cafeteria. Today is beef tips on rice, green beans, a salad, roll, tapioca pudding, and beverage of choice. The kitchen serves me a large quantity because I'm the most active resident of Evergreen Meadows Senior Community. Most everybody else gets the medium to small quantity. The kitchen staff quickly learns who needs extra salad and pudding and who leaves green beans and rice on their plate.

Harassing The Natives

Now that I'm a resident, I'm allowed to loiter in the hallways, and I frequently do so outside Greta's door, located on the main avenue between assisted living and the dining room. There is a lot of foot traffic. To my left, I see Margaret approaching, pushing her walker. I'm in a frivolous mood and I call her out.

"Young lady," I bellow. "Do you have a hall pass? I think you should be in class, and if you don't have permission to be out here, you'll have to report to the principal's office!"

Margaret is shorter than five feet, I'm taller than six. She has a curved spine and has to turn her head upwards to stare me in the eye.

"I think you can stick it in your…" Margaret pauses for a beat, then continues. "…ear. You can stick it in your ear!"

She is clearly considering a different orifice, but chooses a more discrete option. I'm shocked, I say. SHOCKED to hear such a big thing come from such a small woman. We smile and she is on her way.

Later she stops by to ask forgiveness for her spicy response. Janell steps in, saying "Margaret, you said exactly the right thing. You're Mark's new best friend." I'm being ganged up on by the women—deservedly so.

When she's not telling me to stuff it, Margaret is morose. Her body is failing and she is ready for the Lord to call her home, a common euphemism for a merciful death. I kneel down at her table in the dining hall, place my left arm on the back of her chair, my right hand on her arm, and I look her in eyes. She has my full attention and I listen as she tells me what she hopes for.

Once she told me about the "Blue Top Restaurant." Her husband would take her there on special occasions. I gather they had a passionate relationship. She is refined and doesn't share details, but I'll bet with a bit of prodding I could get some steamy tales. I resolve to take her back to the restaurant as a special treat.

When I find it on the internet, it has a one-star review with pictures of a semi-abandoned building with peeling paint and surrounded by chain link fences. It is a grimy shadow of the restaurant she remembers and I cancel my plans. The Blue Top Restaurant has a better existence in Margaret's memories.

I'm becoming a personality at Evergreen Meadows Senior Community. I hang out in the halls, I play Rummikub in the community room, I eat meals. I have an expansive sense of humor and they enjoy my enthusiasm. I have friends here.

On Saturdays, sons and daughters take my friends out to dinner. I sit outside the front door, enjoy the sun, and wave as they drive off. If I'm still sitting outside when they return, residents will often join me. Sons and daughters say their goodbyes and go back to their lives.

I have the pleasure of enjoying a sunset with someone who knows how few sunsets remain to them and how precious every morning can be. We don't talk about their lunch or their children.

My Muse

When I'm not hanging out with Greta, I write. I'm working on my second science fiction novel. But the characters are elusive, and I'm unable to force the book into existence. My muse is supposed to help me with this heavy lift, but is apparently vacationing at Mount Helicon. (This is prime season to be handing out laurel staffs to the local shepherds. Plus, the skiing is awesome.) I write a sentence, then delete the sentence. Electronic word processors have spared me from having to purchase whiteout in bulk.

Early in my writing career, I assumed my muse would appear in a form similar to Venus De Milo—but with arms. Standing in a green pasture, she would strum on a harp while narrating outlines of Pulitzer-Prize winning novels. I would sit in a comfortable chair and transcribe her words while the literary world clamored to offer me fame and fortune.

Yes. Well. Apparently not the case.

Instead, my muse has a Master's degree in harassment with a minor in karate. She wears coveralls, carries a clipboard in her left hand and a ball-point pen in her right. She clicks the pen to punctuate her words. She is not serene.

She unexpectedly pops in one afternoon after Drum Fit exercise class. I am staring out the window, watching Zero the dog chase the same squirrel he chases every day. I don't realize muse is here until she slaps me upside my head with a round-house, full-arm swing that catches me just on the top of my skull, pitching me forward and leaving a bruise. If I'd been wearing a baseball cap it would've flown across the room.

"Welcome back," I say. I rub my head and stare at her with a peeved look I learned from Gladice.

"Why are you ignoring me?" she asks. I assume her pronouns are she/her, but since she is incorporeal, they could be anything. "I've provided you with a wealth of writing prompts, but you complain and do nothing."

"Writing prompts?" I ask. "I haven't seen anything from you lately."

"Gladice? Greta?" she says. "Red Chair? Bingo? Who do you think got you this living situation? God is capricious, but he does listen to prayers. Mine at least. And by the way, you're welcome. I'll check up in a week."

She disappears in a theatrical poof of smoke, leaving me with a room full of stories waiting for my attention. Now that I know how to see them, they become insistent, crowding around like puppies at mealtime. Science fiction will have to wait until I transcribe the puppies to paper.

Unexpectedly, I have access to new perspectives from an older generation. This is the generation who told me I needed a haircut, who told me Satan inspired the Beatles, and who told me astronauts drank Tang. It's also the generation that changed my diapers, let me use the family car, and currently occupies the highest seats of government.

Our Shared Experience

Aging parents are a common topic among my peers. We worry about them and forget to connect their present lives with their past. Taken as a snapshot of this final chapter of their lives, they are simply "old people." Taken as a sum of their whole lives, they present a vibrant community of history and humor.

I'm honored to be welcomed by Greta's community.

Furnished Apartment

When Janell and I were first dating, I lived on a three-season porch. In Minnesota. In winter. With no heat or insulation on the large windows.

I had a space heater: one of those gray metal 1,500-watt devices with the two chrome bars attached to the front to prevent fires should the unit tip over on its face. This brave little toaster may have aspired to start a fire; instead, it tried its best to warm the room, but was no match for the high thermal conductivity of the wrap-around glass.

The heater pointed directly at my pillow with no discernible effect. For a bed, I had a two-inch foam pad and some sheets. Possibly a quilt. I was not big on home furnishings.

This sub-standard sleeping arrangement repelled Janell, but she was attracted by my youthful exuberance. Forty years later, I'm still exuberant, but room 202 of Evergreen Meadows Senior Community was going to be furnished differently. Once again, I realize how fortunate I was to marry her and put her in charge of improving my common sense.

Janell's sister agrees to loan us furnishings. This furniture, including a bed and table, are located in a Milwaukee storage unit. All I have to do is move it one hundred and fifty-five miles from Milwaukee to Stevens Point and return it when we are done.

"No problem," I confidently assure Janell. "Our car has a tow hitch, we can rent a 6x12 trailer from U-Haul, I'll drive down, load up, and we're set!" I am all enthusiasm, but no experience.

My Theology

I've written a bit about my theology. I believe we aren't prepared to understand God. Here's an analogy: I raise chickens in my backyard.

They are sweet and have their squabbles and sometimes I have to discipline or separate them.

But they don't understand what happens in the larger house standing next to their coop.

"It's important you understand the payment of electric bills," I say to the gathered flock. They circle around me, but I can tell their attention is brief; a fly or the discovery of a worm will soon distract them. "Electricity enables us to use the internet, which provides us access to the vast knowledge of the World Wide Web. The web provides me with information on how to keep you healthy, as well as the performance of the stock market."

They get bored and wander off. They lack the context and vocabulary to understand electricity and its related wonders. They also don't possess the cognitive skills to understand the internet or World Wide Web.

I suspect I have the same relationship with God. God thinks I'm sweet, but oh-so-dumb. I find it necessary to describe "him" in terms of a human presence, complete with arms, legs, and emotions because I can't wrap my head around a totally abstract God. "He" (she? it? them? they?) can't explain to me how I am wrong because I don't have the cognitive skills.

So I become distracted by flies and worms and erratically wonder how God works. But I will never attain cosmic wisdom.

God is a Bartender

Instead of becoming overwhelmed with my inadequacies, I make something up. I choose to think of God as a good-natured fellow, with St. Peter as his trusty side kick and administrative assistant.

God seems to have taken an interest in my trip to Milwaukee.

At this moment, God is serving drinks at his heavenly-themed pub. St. Peter, as is normal, is trying to manage God's omnipotent and omnipresent schedule.

"Pete!" God exclaims, looking up at St. Peter while he fills a pint with a cream stout on nitro. "Did you catch what Mark agreed to do?"

"Which one?" asks St. Peter.

"The one headed to Milwaukee," replies God. "Gospel Mark has the day off."

"It's on the list," St. Peter wearily points to the clipboard he has been carrying for the last millennium. He turns to the second page. "It's on line 1,048,323,499,092:"Mark drives to Milwaukee to pick up furniture."

"Right. That's the one." God delivers the pint to the prostitute sitting at the end of the bar (Everyone is welcome here). "Let's add some color to his life."

"You have better things to do," St. Peter flips back to page one, line one and begins to recite. God cuts him off.

"Yes, and we'll get to that. In the meantime, this newly arrived collection of poor in spirit and persecuted deserve a good laugh." God winks at the meek and mourning sitting next to the prostitute. "Can't inherit the kingdom of heaven without some good humor."

St. Peter contemplates the wineglass in front of him. He looks up at God, but God is telling jokes and giving his new friends reasons to rejoice and be glad.

Adventures In Moving

The U-Haul dealer believes I know what I am doing and leaves me to attach the trailer. I back the car up and try to lift the hitch onto the ball. I lift with my legs (not my back). Can't do it. Too heavy.

"Hmmm…," I ponder. Nobody else is around except the trailer and the car. They look at each other, snigger, and look back at me, feigning attentiveness. They aren't talking.

God nudges the pure in heart, who is still adjusting to being able to see God. Pure-in-heart laughs nervously, takes a tentative sip, and watches the show on the big screen at the end of the bar.

The car has a jack for changing a tire. Perfect. I jack up the trailer, back up the car, drop the jack, the hitch goes on the ball. Problem solved. The jack goes back in the car. I connect the safety chain, drive around the parking lot once to check my work. Everything stays attached, so I start off for Milwaukee!

Johari's Window

There is a graphic counseling device called Johari's Window. It is used to help people understand their relationship with themselves and others. It is a grid of four squares: two rows, two columns. The columns are "Known to self" and "Not known to self." The rows are "Known to others" and "Not known to others." Each of the cells contains something revealing about the person or situation. Here is an example:

	Known To Others	**Not Known To Others**
Known To Self	I am driving to Milwaukee with a 6x12 trailer.	I am getting low on gas.
Not Known To Self	Janell knows I should be less than confident.	I have neglected to tighten the hitch latch to the ball.

Remember; God is omniscient, so this doesn't apply to them/her/him/three-in-one. By association, everyone at the bar knows all as well, so they see the approaching punchline.

Cruising down the highway at 65 mph (My rearview mirror reflects WARNING: DO NOT EXCEED 55 MPH WITH THIS TRAILER) I question my pre-flight checklist. Did I put on the safety chains? (Yes). Did the trailer tires have air? (Yes). Was the trailer empty? (Yes). Did I tighten the hitch latch to the ball? (Possibly not. Sure I did. Can't remember. Yes. No.) Perhaps I should check.

Ahead is a rest stop - perfect for checking hitches. I turn smoothly and decelerate. Unfortunately, the Wisconsin Department of Transportation has neglected their maintenance on this rest area. There are potholes. BIG potholes filled with water. Potholes so frequent and so large they are impossible to dodge. I hit one, then a second. I look in the rear-view mirror and see the trailer lurching and bucking behind me. I feel a tug; the trailer has clearly jumped off the ball and is now free to run me down or puncture my gas tank. I sloooowly come to a stop, trying not to irritate this 6x12 untethered monster trailing my car.

I roll to a stop and breathe. Everything is still on the road. The trailer is still behind me. I walk to the back, expecting broken sheet metal and leaking gasoline.

The trailer tongue is in the dirt. It has wedged itself under the car and come to the end of the safety chain. I don't smell gas and there aren't any unsightly bruises in the bumper. Glorious! All I need to do is put the trailer back on the ball and we are good to go. So simple.

But the trailer is wedged under the bumper. I try to lift the car off the trailer tongue. I lift with my legs. Can't do it. Like deja-vue, I remember the jack. I lift the rear of the car, freeing the trailer from its entrapment.

Chock, Jack, and Block

Chock is a funny word. It's a noun, it's a wedge, and comes in sets of four. They are used to keep the wheels of cars or trailers from unexpectedly rolling. In a pinch, you can use a brick, or a stump, or a rock. I had neglected to chock the wheels on the trailer before lifting the car.

The newly freed trailer rolls backwards. I can only watch in dismay—I know enough to not step behind the trailer (empty weight: 1,920 pounds). Today, I am a lucky boy. The chains are still attached; the car is still in contact with the ground; the trailer reaches the end of its tether and stops with a jerk. I resume breathing.

This will be easy to solve. I disconnect the safety chains and pull the car forward. I jack up the trailer, then back the car to the hitch. Only this time, I don't jack the trailer up far enough. With barely a nudge, the jack falls backward and the trailer again rolls towards the ditch. I stupidly watch. "Stupidly" because I should have chocked the wheels; "watch" because that's the sum total of actions available to me.

Three feet of drama later, the trailer stops, but for no good reason. I run to the nearby woods to find a piece of wood small enough for me to lift and large enough to chock a 1,920 pound trailer. With a new appreciation for trailer behavior, I again jack up the tongue and successfully mount the hitch to the ball. I reattach the chains. And yes, I finally lock the trailer to the ball. I return to the freeway.

The entire bar-full of the blessed are trying not to snort beer through their noses. Even the murderer, forgiven for her sins but forevermore guilt-ridden, manages a chuckle. Perhaps there is redemption.

Gas. Rain.

My car displays the distance I can drive in miles. It does this by multiplying the calculated miles-per-gallon times gallons of gas in the tank. It's a computer trick added by an intern Honda hired for the summer. His name is Stephen. *Available Range* doesn't really tell me anything more than what I could observe by looking at the gas gauge at the bottom of the speedometer, but adding it to the car was the crowning act of Stephen's college degree.

For me, I am happy with analog: when the gas needle gets to the last quarter of the tank, I should fill up. That's where the needle is now, so I should do this. I watch signs for a freeway exit with a gas station.

God grabs the remote and hands it to one of the merciful. "Turn up the volume," he/she/they laugh. The merciful hesitates; after all, they are merciful and worries how this will change this mortal's fate. God sees the hesitation and offers a promise of reward; "Don't worry, I got this." The merciful looks at St. Peter, who shakes his head in disbelief, but also nods assurance. The merciful turns up the volume.

It is raining, so I turn on the wipers. First at intermittent, then low speed, then high as the abrupt storm obliterates the view of other cars and roadside features. The rain has enough force to bounce back in the air when it hits the hood of my car. I can't see the exit signs.

With the trailer dragging along behind, the car is getting half the normal MPG I expect. With a curse, I see Stephen's available range is a single digit. I have nine miles to buy gas. Oops—now I have eight. Seven. This trailer must have its brakes on. Stephen would be excited to see his internship project has dialed my anxiety up to eleven.

I am curious whether Stephen programmed his available range computer to stop at zero, or will he display negative numbers? If it goes to negative numbers, I will know Stephen has a warped sense of humor. It means he wrote a special routine which recognizes IF (I am beyond hope) THEN {make fun of me}.

The range goes to zero, then remains zero. Stephen has no sense of humor.

The obvious conclusion to this part of the story sees me walking five miles to a gas station in a pounding rain, wondering what seam of my raincoat is going to start leaking next. But my God is a merciful god. Or he must not have pushed my cream-pie button hard enough, because I turn off at the next exit and can see an (*open*) gas station. *Maybe the Merciful handed the remote to St. Peter who toned things down a bit.*

I don't know if Stephen programmed in a margin of safety, or how accurate his sensor data was, or if he simply did the calculation with no concern for human fragility. I am tempted to circle the gas pump until I truly sputter to a stop, but I am done tempting The Fates and fill up the tank. No more drama, please.

"Okay everyone," God says. "Happy hour is over. Orientation starts in fifteen minutes." (Or 15 eons. Time is fluid in God's kingdom.) Everyone, including those hungering for righteousness (manifested as free bar snacks) head for the door.

Somehow, things are suddenly quieter for me. The rest of the trip isn't worth writing about. I pick up the furniture; I return to Stevens Point; I unload the trailer; I return the U-Haul; I have an apartment with furnishings —an enormous step above the mattress and space heater of my youth. Janell is happy. I am happy.

Many people of faith look for evidence of God by praying for miracles. In my life, I've had way too many lucky brushes with fate to require proof. I'm not sure what God is, but I know I should be drowned or crushed or choked or out of gas or pushing a trailer out of a ditch.

Instead, I'm here in Stevens Point, telling jokes to my Mother-In-Law. For that, I feel an immense sense of grace and forgiveness.

The Red Chair

We all create ghostly echoes.

Some are formal and intentional: tombstones, memorials, buildings, statues.

Some are transitory and mysterious: your sense of being watched, strange sounds in the house, objects disappearing and reappearing, dreams of conversations with the deceased.

Some are the pressure of things we leave behind: clothing, fishing rods, photos, cremation ashes, toothbrushes, Facebook accounts, furniture.

I have a ghostly echo in my living room.

The Pile

Our apartment at Evergreen Meadows Senior Community includes access to a security cage for large items. It's in the basement parking garage, next to a disordered pile of wheelchairs, walkers, assistive toilet devices, and easy lift recliners. I assume former residents left these behind. Former, as in *moved on*. I haven't dug for any history on these items, but I suspect these are no longer useful to the previous owners or their children.

This flotsam rests in an uninteresting pile in an unswept corner of the garage. Nobody comes down here except to retrieve their car. There's no dramatic lighting, creepy features, or ominous soundtrack to warn of a haunting.

This is where I meet the red chair.

Theft of the Red Chair

It's a beautiful day in May and Janell and I return from a bike ride; I store my bike in the basement security cage, then wander over to the pile. Amidst the walkers and wheelchairs is a red leather La-Z-Boy recliner. It is in perfect condition, no rips or worn-through patches. The chair has a large wood lever to control the footrest. Lean back and it unfolds to a horizontal position. Move to sit upright and it folds to a normal chair shape. Its purpose is to make you comfortable; this is why it exists.

The only wear and tear is a discolored area corresponding to the previous owner's head and faded spots on the armrests. Echoes of a past life.

It's easy to see how the chair cradled its owner; late night television supplying unwatched light and unheard sound. Every evening, both chair and owner rested peacefully until one morning when the owner did not greet the sunrise. Maintenance cleaned the apartment but nobody wanted the chair, so they hauled it downstairs. To the pile.

Janell stores her bicycle next to mine and comes over to see what I am looking at. Without any need for imagination, we see the ghost of the chair's owner. It stands behind the chair, one hand possessively stroking the head rest. The ghost, with the eternal desire of those who have moved on, whispers a sales pitch. It has an interest in the well-being of this favorite chair.

"*It's mechanically perfect,*" says the ghost.

The chair behaves like any kennel dog being considered for adoption, straightens its shoulders and looks at us with a hopeful expression.

"*It's valued at $1,800 retail,*" says the ghost.

The chair does its best to hide the dust on its arms and seat.

"*You need such a chair!*" concludes the ghost. It pauses, waiting for our decision.

Janell doesn't hesitate. "Get a dolly; we're taking this upstairs."

Not So Fast

Building Administration for Evergreen Meadows Senior Community knows about this chair; It has a history and a death sentence. The ghost doesn't mention the bedbug infestation and appointment with a dumpster.

If I were the ghost, I would make a similar omission. From the staff, we learn this chair was one of a set; they had already disposed of its partner. Our ghost had seen the future and—like Marley in *A Christmas Carol*—is doing its best to prevent the repeat of that fate. We unknowingly take part in the clandestine rescue of this chair.

Using our best spatial skills, we fit it in the elevator, sneak it to our apartment, and give it a place of prominence in our small living room.

A week later, housekeeping sees the chair and reports its salvation. Administration sends their angel of destruction; Joe from maintenance. The message is clear and final; we must return the chair to suffer its demise. The certification of assisted living facilities does not allow bedbugs; this chair is a carrier and so must be expunged.

It is unfair to paint Administration as the villain in this story. This lone chair threatens the existence of a multi-million dollar senior care facility, closure of which will cause the unemployment of thirty staff and the expulsion of two hundred residents onto the streets. The staff do their best, given the constraints of state licensing guidelines and the boundaries of good common sense. The chair is an innocent victim of government regulation.

Missing from this drama is the actual presence of bedbugs. To sanitize the chair, Maintenance had previously heated it to 200 degrees—bedbugs die at 115 degrees. Like a Greek hero, the chair passed through the gates of hell to gain redemption.

We have sat in this chair for days with no bites. There are no bedbugs. We ignore Administration's warning.

It is only a week after the first warning when I am stopped in the hall. Joe informs me that if I load the chair on a dolly, he will be glad to remove it. He is polite, but this is not a suggestion. The chair must be destroyed; we may not intervene on its behalf. *Bedbugs. State regulations. Employment.*

I have a photograph of Greta sleeping in this chair. She is tucked in with a colorful afghan and has an angelic smile. The chair is at peace; it is fulfilling a destiny. In the corner of our apartment stand the ghost and the chair, looking at us with hopeful eyes. In good conscience I cannot stand by and allow it to be destroyed.

But how?

Hidden Fugitive

Jon, my college roommate, lives nearby. He collects old cars and stray dogs. Actually, his wife collects dogs, Jon collects cars. Dogs and old cars are alike except maintenance of the dogs is a fraction of that of the cars. Jon enters this story with an important asset: he owns a barn.

I wrap the chair in plastic and load it into my car, then show up at Jon's with the chair and a six-pack of beer. I leave with neither. I assure him I will return in a month to retrieve the chair and transport it to my home in Portland. Jon has experienced many years of my unpredictable antics, but agrees to cooperate. Problem solved!

Our apartment is devoid of the chair. We invite Housekeeping to survey the residence. Everything is as it should be.

Only…there are four depressions in the carpet where it stood. An echo.

An Unintended Return

Three weeks later Jon invites us to his home of rambunctious dogs and slumbering cars. Also attending is a frolic of former college roommates. Beer is consumed and old stories are embellished. Sometime between our arrival and the departure of common sense, we decide to move a truck topper from an unmowed patch to an unkempt room in the barn. We perform this like pallbearers carrying a coffin to a grave. It's probable this topper won't move from this resting place for many years—normal for objects in a barn.

Janell doesn't take part in the transport, but she observes the final placement of the topper; It is within eyesight of the chair.

Janell was not pleased about moving the chair to Jon's barn. This was my doing and she unwillingly allowed it to happen. But it is clear she sides with the ghost and the chair, making it three-to-one in favor of the chair residing in front of the television in our room, rather than supplying a spawning facility for mice and pigeons.

I finish with the truck topper and turn to see the ghost and Janell considering the chair.

"I'm getting the car," they say. "We're loading this up and taking it back." I'm unclear who is the "we" in this sentence, but it will include me as part of the lift team. I am also included in the unload team, the dolly team, and the elevator team.

The return of this chair means we must banish Housekeeping. We scrub our own toilet and vacuum our own carpet. It is a slight inconvenience considering the feelings of the chair and the pleasure of employing it as a cozy nest for evening television.

New Home, Same Skill

At the end of our stay at Evergreen Meadows Senior Community, we transport the chair 1,945 miles to our home in Portland, Oregon. The chair is a good traveler: doesn't require bathroom breaks, doesn't shed or bark, will listen to whatever music or audiobook we choose, and doesn't pee on the carpet when we stop at hotels. Positioned in our living room, the chair fulfills its purpose with pleasure, wrapping itself around anyone willing to pause long enough for a pre-bedtime nap.

My younger son, Aaron, came for a visit the other day. He already heard the rumor of the red chair and the history of bedbugs. He experienced his own bedbug episode which resulted in the dumpsterizing of his leather overstuffed lounger.

Aaron regards the red chair much the same way you might regard a roadkill dragged into the house.

"So," he said. He stands somewhat leaned back, hands in pockets. He raises one eyebrow. "This is the chair?"

The chair straightens its shoulders and looks at Aaron with a hopeful expression.

"It's mechanically perfect!" I say. "It's valued at $1,800 retail. We need such a chair!"

Aaron isn't convinced and his posture doesn't change. The chair looks from Aaron to me, hoping for reassurance I'll protect it. I pat the back of the chair. No worries little buddy, nobody is taking you to the dumpster.

Ghosts

Janell and I are downsizing. We don't need furniture for two guest rooms. We don't need a table to seat eight. We don't want a lawnmower, and we don't need a couch and four lounge chairs to watch television. But I'm certain we will still need a red chair. I'm uncertain we have a voice in the decision. The chair is with us until we find it a new home to the ghost's liking. Until then, the chair is in our living room.

I take great comfort knowing a chair can have a spiritual guardian. If something as insignificant as a mass-produced piece of furniture is cared for, then what about me? Or you? I can only hope for such an advocate when I have bedbugs and become destined for disposal.

Nickel Bingo

On Sunday, a weekly activity guide appears in my mailbox. Fitness class is on Monday at 1:00 p.m. The Catholics among us recite the Rosary at 2:30 on Wednesdays. Ice cream is just before the Rosary.

That's all very nice, but how we *long* for bingo night.

Important Things

Nickel Bingo is every Thursday at 6:00 p.m.

There are two notable parts of this sentence. Lesser, but still significant, is the time: Nickel Bingo happens at 6 p.m. Activities occurring past 5:00 p.m. are *late-evening*. ~~Supper~~ ~~Dinner~~ Supper is served from 4:30 to 5:30 p.m.; after that, the halls become the domain of the night owls. Any resident gatherings after six feel surreptitious. Walk unannounced into one of the activity rooms and you may find residents quietly playing Rummikub, but that's just to avert suspicion; when you move out of earshot, they will resume plotting world domination.

Before living here, these late-nighters huddled around the corner table in a seedy bar, speaking in lowered voices and pausing their planning when the server came by to refill drinks. After I have lived here for a month, they trust me a bit. But they still change conversation when I approach.

At six o'clock on Thursday evenings, the late-nighters forego Rummikub and move to the Independent Dining Room for *nickel bingo*.

Nickel Bingo

Nickel Bingo is the second notable thing in the above sentence. There are *other* games during the week, notably candy bingo and jewelry bingo, but these are minor-league compared to nickel bingo. If you win at candy or jewelry bingo, you get to choose a piece of candy (or a piece of jewelry). But, *you don't put anything in the cup to play*. You can show up empty-handed and still win. The bingo sharks participate in these lesser events, but only as a side to the big event on Thursday evening.

Very few men show up for candy or jewelry bingo. I asked the activity coordinators if there is ever gun, fishing lure, or whiskey bingo. (answer: *no!*) I've thought of organizing an underground bingo association for the men; the poorly lit basement garage would be ideal for a cigar-smoking, scotch-drinking Friday night game. So far, I've abstained from instigating this clandestine event. I don't want to be the cause (or subject) of an *official memo* on inappropriate evening activities.

Official Memos

Official memos come from the Facility Director and appear in your campus mail slot; sometimes posted in the elevator. The memo vaguely insinuates a precipitating situation, but the intent is clear:

"Keep it up, buster, and your children will interview other residence halls for your next placement."

Games

In my family, games were a thing to do with your hands while we socialized. In the Ross family, games are serious. "*Are you going to talk, or are you going to play?*" They here to win. After a few rounds, I realize I don't have the level of competitiveness required. So I watch and make irreverent commentary from the sidelines.

Greta will happily play cribbage well past my bedtime. She's quick, recognizes the points for certain combinations of cards and announces her score after a glance. Apparently it's an automatic reflex, like breathing or heart beats or flinching away from the strong coffee I make.

Lately, we've noticed her count is wrong. She accidentally double counts (But not on purpose. Gene would do it to see if we were paying attention.)

Instead of cribbage, I take Greta to community bingo. She misses some of the called numbers, but I back her up. We like hanging out together more than playing bingo.

Bingo Basics

General bingo knowledge will help you understand the drama associated with nickel bingo. I'll make this as brief as possible, after which I'll explain why our quiet little games frequently descend into mayhem.

Explained simply, bingo is a game of drawing a straight line through five random numbers on a grid. A caller selects those numbers, then players mark them if they are on their card. When the marks form a row or column, the player calls out "BINGO." Everyone expresses amazement, and the game is reset.

Players select a bingo card from a stack. I don't believe you can bring your own card. This isn't like pool where you own a custom-made stick. Private cards, at the least, would be a topic of conversation for weeks; at worst, it would be the cause of another *official memo*.

The Player Table

Our players agreed on assigned seating, even though an *official memo* discouraged this behavior. Visitors might consider sitting at the room's periphery to avoid crashing this unspoken tradition. If you can't find a seat, you should just watch, rather than cause a disruption. I earned the position of honored guest and am invited to join one of the regular tables.

Each player has two bingo cards. (I could play more, but two is the norm. And I've learned to stick to the norm. Mostly. Occasionally. *It's complicated*.)

A small bowl sits in the middle of our table. It might be empty or it might contain change. At the beginning of each round, we contribute one nickel per card, placing the coins in the bowl. Two cards, two nickels. Therefore, we call this game nickel bingo. Four people at the table times two cards results in eight nickels in the bowl. Which equals forty cents. Instead of two nickels, we may deposit one dime. If someone deposits a quarter, they can remove fifteen cents.

If I forget my jar of nickels, I sponge off Greta. She's gracious, but I worry this will strain our relationship. Her change includes quarters, dimes, pennies, and sometimes dollar bills. A side note: for God's sake, don't bring foreign currency. This would precipitate another *official memo*.

Before I remove money from the bowl, I am *inordinately* clear about my action and intention. Someone might misconstrue sudden movement. Fortunately, weapons are not allowed in our building.

Game Phase One—The Collection

Before each round of bingo begins, the designated money collector circulates among the tables and gathers coins from each bowl. We assume the collector confirms each table has contributed the correct amount (*but maybe not. More on this in a minute*). Coins are placed at the head table and the bingo caller proceeds.

Collecting fees must be done with efficiency. Everyone waits for the game to begin, but not patiently. Pick up the bowl, count the change. This should be simple enough.

But not so fast...

You might think collection is an inconsequential job, but it is not. An informal and self-designated sub-committee of residents bestows the honor of collector upon an individual. The qualifications are not available for public review anywhere that I've seen, but I believe the main qualifier is squeezing between tightly packed tables, walkers, and wheelchairs. This requires the ability to bend your knees and locomote without support. I am proud to note I was asked to perform this task and discharged my duties with the earnestness of a first-time student council president.

Now—-I propose a conundrum for you to consider. *What is the proper response if the change is not correct for the number of bingo cards visible on the table?*

The obvious strategy would be to ask if everyone has contributed. When I'm fortunate, one member will realize it is time to ante-up and contribute their fair share. Unfortunately, this rarely happens.

It's probable someone miscounted when they made change; a quarter in the bowl is an indicator. Miscounted change is exacerbated by the cumulative arthritis of everyone at the table. Arthritis is when your knuckles grind bone-on-bone. To develop empathy, insert 60-grit sandpaper between each joint in your fingers so it is excruciating to bend them, then wrap each finger in duct-tape so you cannot flex. Now, try to pick up three nickels placed in a small bowl to make change for your quarter.

In all cases, I've found it easiest to agree everything is accurate, then pour this bowl into the general collection. This isn't an IRS audit and the amount to be won is secondary to the win itself. Smile and move on.

During my training to become certified as a bingo money collector, I also learned of the inadvertent donation timing confusion. Here's a scenario:

1. I arrive at the table and develop empathy with the players. I assure them they will win during this round. They assume I am lying to gain their favor, which is true.

2. Someone needs change, most likely for a dollar. I make change from the bingo fees I've already collected.

3. I reach to collect the bowl. In this scenario, someone will object; "You already collected for this round."

I am *certain* I have not collected. But I am only one vote out of five, the other four being the players seated at the table. They assume the bowl contains money for the next round. The act of making change interrupted the normal interaction between players and the collector. Or sadly, their short-term memory is a bit wobbly. Untangling this error is torturous. I tried to reason through a narrative of the collection, but there is no point to this. Again—smile. Move on.

Someone may not contribute or is flustered with the quick flow of money across the table. I learned to carry a supplemental pocket of nickels and make a lightning loan where necessary. *"I've got you covered,"* I tell my new friend. In a few minutes, everyone forgets about the loan, but the friendship remains. I count that as a win.

As you might realize, collections became an issue of major contention and even made it to a topic of discussion at a town hall. Volunteers stepped up with a plan; now we have a collection system inspired by the traditions of the Lutheran Church.

Game Phase Two—The Calling

After the collection, the bingo caller proceeds with the announcing of numbers. Again, let me explain the simple concept, then the nuances that lead to shouting.

Bingo Caller Certification

You might think I am kidding about bingo caller certification. I am not. Depending on location, you may be required to take a class, pass a test, and/or annually renew your license. Search the internet for "bingo certification" for details.

To start, the caller draws one ball from a bucket of 75 and announces the letter/number combination ("G-48. That's GEE…FOUR…EIGHT), then —and this is important—places that ball in a master matrix. With the ball safely in place, the caller repeats the process. The matrix is an easy way to confirm which numbers have been called. Which is important when someone calls…

BINGO!

What could go wrong?

The Caller

Qualities of a good bingo caller include enunciation, volume, and pacing. This is much like an auctioneer, but slower. There is such a thing as lightning bingo—but not here.

Ideally, the caller will draw a ball from the bucket, then call out the number clearly and carefully, pause, repeat the letter and number, place the ball in the matrix, pause, shuffle the balls, and draw another.

However, some callers forget their training and gain bad habits: Speaking softly. Sloppy pronunciation. Calling too fast. When auditioning a caller, we favor experience as pastor, square-dance caller, sports announcer, elementary school teacher, or game-show host. Unfortunately, the qualification of the caller is not the only chaotic force in action.

Pacing is every bit as important as volume and enunciation. As we age, our brains suffer a reduction in processing speed. When I was twenty-years-old, I could do math in my head. I could also perform deep-knee bends while lifting seventy-pound weights. Forty years later, math takes longer and my knees support less weight. Pausing between bingo calls gives everyone a chance to hear the number, parse the number, check both bingo cards, slide the plastic cover, wiggle the cover if it sticks, confirm the number with a neighbor, check for a bingo pattern, and re-focus to prepare for the next call. Bingo players don't like it when callers move too fast.

Rattle

About those damn bingo balls. They are plastic; every time the caller stirs the bucket of balls, they generate noise akin to a ball-bearing factory. It masks human speech. If they don't pause long enough between calling the number and stirring the balls, we hear the following…

"O-63…that's O- (RATTLERATTLERATTLE). The next number is B-3. That's B- (RATTLERATTLERATTLE)."

RATTLERATTLERATTLE causes a cascade of secondary noise, caused by one or more calls to repeat the last number, followed by some of the bingo players repeating the number (out of sync, so the response is also confused) followed by the bingo caller demanding silence, which is followed by more bingo players again asserting the latest number simultaneous to a different group of players asking if it was a different number, followed by the caller repeating the number, followed by someone asking if that is the last number or the next number. Simultaneously, there is background rumbling about the caller being inaudible or the players needing to pay better attention.

Also problematic are outsiders: relatives, children, nursing staff, janitors. Relatives and children are the worst, as they have no respect for the sanctity of the game in progress. Typically, they appear at the door, squeal, and call out; "GRANDMA! WE'RE HERE!" They invade our sanctuary en masse, surround their relative and talk loudly about their *car trip* and *how good it is to see them* and *how big the kids have grown* and *we have this pie we baked for you* and *what's going on here* and *Oh, I love bingo* and *we should join in.*

I'm enthusiastic about visitors. They brighten up everyone's day. But *gawdammit*, we're trying to play **bingo** here. ***Nickel Bingo!***

Likewise, the nursing staff will sometimes stop by for blood pressure and pulseOx. They truly are heroes and wrangle medications with grace and care. But the brief interruption in game play means possibly missed numbers, causing one or more calls to repeat the last number, followed by some bingo players repeating the number … and so on.

The maintenance team tries to be quiet, but sometimes they vacuum in the next room. A vacuum cleaner produces "white noise," and it masks the bingo caller's voice. One must choose: clean carpet, or bingo.

Hearing

If the caller enunciates, projects, and paces—and someone's kid isn't banging out chopsticks on the piano—then it is reasonable to assume everything will go smoothly.

By age 80, it's not uncommon to experience a hearing loss of 50% in the frequency range of the human voice. Roughly one-third of the bingo players have some level of dementia, a symptom being confusion and agitation when dealing with the cacophony of many people talking at once.

Do you wonder how this feels? Try balancing your checkbook while teaching a freshman band class. Add in a persistent five-year-old learning to tie their own shoes. Formally, this is cognitive overload. Informally this is *Can you all just be quiet for ten minutes? Oh my gawd I'm getting a headache!*

By the way, good table mates look out for each other. After I scan my bingo cards, I stealthily check my neighbor's cards and politely point out any numbers they missed. Done quietly, this is a gesture of kindness.

Game Phase Three—BINGO

It eventually happens. Sometimes from another table. Sometimes from my table. Sometimes I double-take at my card and hear myself yell **BINGO**!

There are three winning patterns: Five in a row, five in a column, and five diagonally. Sometimes, we have three additional patterns: four corners, picture frame, and the high-stakes *blackout*. (more about blackout in a minute) Some callers try additional patterns (i.e. postage stamp, two lines, small diamond) but approval is mixed.

Upon hearing bingo, the caller pauses the game and verifies the winner.

An experienced caller will remind players *not* to clear their board until the bingo is confirmed. If a bingo isn't confirmed, the confusion quotient of the room will rise. Any player who mistakenly cleared their board will request a re-call of all the drawn numbers, but that takes time and is not popular.

Confirming a bingo is mechanically easy. The winning player reads out loud the numbers comprising their bingo, the caller confirms those numbers were actually called, and if in agreement, the caller announces a winning bingo. To the winner goes the nickels and everyone resets their bingo cards.

Sometimes it isn't easy. As in all steps of bingo, problems appear during the implementation. The concept of "out loud" has various interpretations with multiple variables, including speed of delivery and volume of the player. But…maybe the caller's hearing isn't as good as it used to be. Maybe other players are chatting/gossiping/remarking at how close *they* were to winning. Maybe the caller's memory for numbers isn't 100%. It happens, but hopefully not often and hopefully not to you more than once. There are a limited number of hours available to us, so pay attention.

Blackout Bingo

Each evening bingo session includes ten rounds with the standard row/column/diagonal pattern. As mentioned above, these games cost one nickel per card. There is an additional, final round which uses a blackout pattern—cover **all** windows on the card. The cost per card doubles to *ten cents per card*. The table ante doubles from forty cents to eighty cents. Our bingo room has space for seven tables, so winning blackout bingo is a big payout—-over FIVE DOLLARS!

Blackout bingo takes longer than standard row/column/diagonal patterns, but the suspense is *killer!* I feel my blood pressure rise as I watch the card approach 100% coverage. Several times someone else calling **BINGO** has crushed my fantasy of a big payout. *Dammit!*

Game Phase Four–PAYOUT

I've won several times! A victory dance is tempting. I would beat my chest, throw my winning bingo card across the room and shout "**I DOMINATE! I AM THE BINGO JEDI MASTER! COWER IN FEAR, ALL WHO BEHOLD ME!**" I haven't done this. My knees are not up to dancing around. My older table mates would be ill-advised to beat their chests, considering any history of heart trouble. Finally, throwing anything across the room is likely to poke someone's eye out. Surely an official memo will be the result.

When I win, I revel in the momentary endorphin rush of seeing a pile of change pour into my bingo change jar. I tell my table friends how much fun that was and how surprised I am to win. Then I get ready for the next round.

Two or More Winners

Normally, one person wins each round, but sometimes two (or more) people win at the same time. (The odds of winning bingo is a fascinating subject if you are a statistician or math professor. Look it up on the internet. The rest of us should leave the math geeks in peace).

When multiple **BINGO!**s are confirmed, winners split the prize. As a money collector, it is my job to perform this split. There are two strategies I use to accomplish this accounting feat of derring-do.

- Use math.
- Use eyeball.

There's a secret I learned, and I'll tell you if you promise not to make a big damn deal about it.

Here's the secret: Where I live, *nobody cares how much they won.*

I divide up the money in mostly equal piles. I pour that money into the winner's pouch or jar already containing an uncounted amount of change; there is no accounting trail or software involved. The thrill of the win counts. Delaying the start of the next game is a buzz kill.

Cheating at bingo

We're all pretty sure James cheats. He wins *a lot*—at least, more than he should. I think I figured out how he does it. James sits with his back to a wall so no one can look over his shoulder. He uses small picture easels to hold his two bingo cards upright (Everyone else positions their cards flat on the table).

Here's the trick: In his mind, he combines these two cards into one, doubling his chances of a matching number. When he calls bingo and reads back his numbers, he may read the first number from the first card, then the second number from the *second* card, the third number from the first (or second) card, and so-on.

I have two considerations about this. First, James is showing advanced math skills by converting from a two-dimensional matrix to a three-dimensional array. That's impressive stuff and I'm loath to call him on his adept transformations.

Second, James may not realize he's cheating. Our brains are masters of rerouting around malfunctioning synapses. James may simply adapt to a brain injury sustained on a naval destroyer or army tank. I find it unappreciative to dismiss this level of error-correction as simple cheating.

Either way, I gain nothing by destroying the elated mood surrounding an evening of nickel bingo. I'm spending no more energy on policing James.

Getting Older

Bingo isn't a metaphor for life or how to be an effective manager at work. It's just a game. But it's a game with friends. That's all that matters.

I find it curious we need games to help us socialize. But I try not to overthink it; I'm just here to get to know these people I'm living with. That's enough.

Pedicure

I am sitting in a robotic massage chair, my feet are in a bucket of water; Greta is in a similar predicament in the massage chair next to me. The other women in the mani-pedi shop try not to point and laugh; they aren't trying very hard.

I don't care what they think. I'm having a moment with Greta.

Greta likes to look good. Her hair is coiffed and she's always been a spiffy dresser. Her fingernails and toenails are trimmed, polished, and painted. Greta is a classy woman.

In contrast, I have curated the look of someone who just stepped out of the woods. I trim my nails with a Swiss army knife, my pants are ripped in non-fashionable places, and I wear a shirt when I must.

Greta goes to the hair stylist at Evergreen Meadows, but they don't do toenails or fingernails. Community members get together on Tuesday afternoons and pull out a box of expired nail enamel, but nobody is trimming cuticles, exfoliating or de-callusing. It's mani-pedi lite. (That may not be the technical terms for this type of thing, but mani-pedi's are not my field of expertise.)

I create educational videos for LinkedIn Learning. I demonstrate assembling electronics to an overhead camera; similar to a baking show with an overhead mirror. Nobody wants to look at my dirty fingernails so my producer, Raye, insists I get a manicure. Sometimes I forget.

"Oh look, we have a delay in filming," Raye tells me. She's being polite. "You have just enough time to run over to the nail salon and spruce things up."

I head off to clean and trim my nails, push the cuticles around, make things pretty. No nail polish, please. I do what my producer says —it's good policy. I have received manicures and I have the sponges and buffing pads necessary for the ordeal.

Today, Greta's toenails and fingernails need attention. Janell is normally the designated caretaker on girlie things, but she takes a schadenfreude attitude, volunteers me, then watches as I squirm. I lock my self-inflicted notions of manhood in a box, make an appointment at "Josephine's Nail Salon" and load Greta and myself in the car.

The toughest part of a manicure + pedicure is knowing when to talk. When I get the oil changed in the car, I surrender the keys, exchange a joke with the manager, grab a bag of free popcorn, and camp out with my email. Manicures are a different event; I don't have any good jokes about fingers, there is no popcorn, and I can't check my email because my fingers are busy getting soaked, buffed, or trimmed. Pedicures are another thing; what do I say to someone who is shaving off my calluses, digging out schmutz from under my toenails, and massaging my insteps. Do we discuss soap operas? (I don't watch any). Modern Philosophy as espoused by Descartes? (I think not).

This time, I don't have that problem; Greta is always chatty and we fall into easy conversation. I occupy myself by figuring out the mystical icons on the control panel in the armrest, providing Greta with the benefit of my newly acquired mastery of the massage chair. I've had more relaxing massages from pneumatic jackhammers.

Earlier, Greta chose nail polish for both of us; a small bottle labeled "Valentine Fuchsia." From what I can tell, it is just Rust-Oleum Ford Red automotive engine enamel but in a smaller bottle. It would take a lot of these little bottles to cover an engine block.

After my feet and hands have been sanded and prepped, the painting begins. The manicurist skips a coat of primer before applying Valentine Fuchsia. She is quick and efficient and has five fingers completed when Greta interjects;

"Oh, ick," Greta says. She's looking at my painted fingernails. "That color is too red. I'm going to pick something different." She paws through the box of Rust-Oleum bottles and comes out with a more conservative pink.

I now have a problem which will compound itself in the coming days. I can stop and switch to match Greta's choice, but this means enduring the grinding necessary to remove the current color. I elect to continue with

Valentine Fuchsia for my remaining fifteen nails. The manicurist irradiates my fingers with army-surplus plutonium and the polish becomes heat-resistant and immune to chipping. Those are qualities of good engine paint, so I assume that is true here as well.

Manicures and pedicures aren't unpleasant; unlike dental work, giving blood, or a vasectomy. Greta and I laugh at the absurdity of it all, then go to Culver's for a treat of frozen custard. The server at Culver's gives my fingers a glance, then takes our order. I can tell there is something slightly askew about our interaction, but don't spend time puzzling it out.

Three days later, we attend a funeral for a friend of Greta's from her early married days. Funerals are a convenient way to catch up on old friendships between those who are still standing. Or sitting. Or at least breathing. The after-funeral reception is happening at the local VFW, which means there is a cafeteria, a formal meeting room, a display case with war memorabilia, and a bar. I've never seen a VFW that didn't have all of these rooms.

I help Greta get comfortable at a table with her friends, make sure everyone has a cup of coffee, then fade into the background. The conversation is about people and events I have never known, so I wander off to the bar.

Bikers and other toughs fill this crowded bar; all former army grunts who believe an occasional bar fight is just good, clean fun. I have the sense to order a generic beer (no craft beers here), which costs me a buck and comes in an eight-ounce glass with an etched logo. I extend my hand to pick up the glass from the bar; the bartender looks at the glass, then my hand, then at me.

I forgot about the nail polish.

If these patrons beat me to a pulp for being a drag-queen-elitist-hack, I won't be able to drive Greta back home, so I need to reframe this situation before I run out of teeth. I play the favorite son-in-law card.

"My mother-in-law chose this color," I say. "She needed a companion and all her friends were busy. Otherwise she would have been lonely."

I'm thankful I'm wearing close-toed shoes. Birkenstocks would have not only confirmed my elitist politics, but also exposed my painted nails. This sort of thing is standard behavior in my hometown of Portland, Oregon, but that's 1,900 miles to the west. In Portland, if you are a man wearing fingernail polish, you are also probably wearing a wig and a sequined dress. You may be late for a city council meeting, which is a problem because you are *on* city council. Possibly *running* the meeting because you are the mayor.

But we're not in Kansas, or Portland, anymore. The bikers gathered around me say nothing. This could go wrong.

God smiles at his little joke, then sends Greta into the bar. She sidles up next to me; the bikers part and let her through.

"Hi Marky," she says. "Did you buy me a beer?"

"Gentlemen, this is Greta, my favorite-mother-in-law," I say. "Greta, please show them your nail polish. Please."

Greta looks at me as if *I'm* the one losing my mind, but produces her fingernails. Our colors aren't exactly the same, but similar enough to have come from the same hardware store.

Motherhood is a strong card to play and it works. The bikers aren't going to challenge Greta (nobody wants to get dressed down by an honored citizen half their height and a third of their weight.) I take a healthy chug of beer and burp; good-old-boy tactics.

I bought Greta that beer and stuck around while she drank it. I had no loss of blood and was able to drive her home. Maybe I'm being overly-dramatic (I am), but at the time, there were a lot of large men who were not wearing nail polish. There was one of me. Add Greta and there were two of us with paint.

Tolerance

I grew up in St. Paul, Minnesota with an entitled attitude gained from living in a big city. I then went to school in Menomonie, Wisconsin, a small town of 12,000. It was only a few days before I offended one of my classmates by suggesting farmers were bumpkins.

“Don’t make fun of farmers with your mouth full,” he informed me. He was right. It was one of those unexpected lessons I learned at college.

Greta was forever willing to love those people around her, even when loving was a hard task. If I had things to do over again, I would try to follow her example and look for the good in everyone I encounter. Greta set a high bar on this one.

I require remedial sessions now and again. Portland tends to the liberal side of things, but I remind myself I live in a political bubble. If the VFW can see clear to my wearing Valentine Fuchsia, certainly I can seek to embrace their view of the world as well.

At Greta’s funeral, I’ll proudly wear fingernail polish in honor of the lesson she taught me. The next time I’m at the auto-parts store, I’ll ask for a bottle of red paint and a small brush.

Hallways

There are seven hallways in the residence where I live; three are in the assisted living wing, three are in the independent wing, and one is in the memory wing. Each hallway services six or more rooms. Each room has a door with a small cubby that invites personal expression. Most cubbies post pictures of Jesus or Mary. Many feature ceramic dogs or cats (but not both). There are plants and flags and war memorabilia and wind chimes and drawings by grandchildren.

A few display artwork created by the occupant; our neighbor Jan paints mandala patterns on rocks. Dave Smith, a professor, dabbled in an abstract type of art he described as *Scarabocchio*—Italian for *scribble*. His door was a wild collage of politics, opinions, and multi-colored doodles. It screamed I AM ECCENTRIC, I AM PROUD OF IT, IT IS WHO I AM. When you are in Stevens Point, Wisconsin, you can visit his museum.

I've seen no lawn flamingos, neon beer signs, dancing hula girls, gumball machines, coin-operated video games, or historical plaques.

A few cubbies host bird houses. There are no birds flying loose in our building and so the houses are empty. But the excursion bus makes a weekly visit to a shopping mall with a pet store. It's a wonder we don't have a population of feral budgies.

For our cubby, I considered an inflatable flappy-arm guy like you see at tire and furniture stores. At 20 feet tall, this would crowd against the eight-foot ceiling, plus the fan might generate more noise than my neighbors will tolerate. Slightly more practical, Fleet Farm sells a target-practice deer with a replaceable core. We live at the end of the hall, but setting up an indoor archery range would precipitate an *official memo*.

Until I act otherwise, we host a Buddha. This isn't because we're Buddhists; A garden Buddha was in our borrowed household items, and it seems fair to offer equal representation for other faiths.

Navigation

This story is about my time spent in Wisconsin, but in other worlds, my parents finished their lives in a residence community in Duluth, Minnesota.

My father experienced difficulties navigating the halls. There were three routes to the dining room, each with additional hallways leading to other wings of the building. Every route was the same color. There were no maps on the walls. He got lost and frustrated and, as a result, never explored his building.

In old European cities, streets have names, but street signs are rare. On your first trip from the hotel to the restaurant, you will get lost and your only hope is landmarks. In Venice, my hotel was a right turn marked by a purple umbrella above the panetteria. In Cortona, I went to the main plaza, turned right at the church steps and climbed the steepest road that did not pass the gelato vendor. In Japan, I kept the window with persimmons to the right, walked towards the cash machine and opened the door of my Ryokan, which had a sticker from the band AC/DC.

If I were king of the world, I would hire an iconographer for every senior residence design team. They would comb thrift stores for unusual objects and post them at every corner in the hall: umbrella, cross, bicycle, snow sled, moose head, sailboat, water ski, flowers, train set, wooden spoons, mixing bowl. Wings of the building wouldn't have numbers or letters (Wing A. Wing B…). They would be destinations: California, New York, Florida, Canada, Germany, Australia. Each artifact in each wing would reflect that location: palm trees, subways, alligators, snow, lederhosen, kangaroos. No words, just pictures and objects and colors.

If you need a local example, take a tour of Epic Systems Incorporated Intergalactic Headquarters in Verona, Wisconsin. Staff offices are in themed buildings: the Barn, Emerald City, Wizard's Academy, the Treehouse, or Deep Space. Visitors navigate the expansive campus by identifying the desired theme, then following signs. I would love to tell friends I work on the third floor of Captain Nemo's submarine; just follow the giant octopus.

With a few modifications, my father would step out of his room, look for the bicycle, turn left at the alligator, go straight until he was in Germany.

He realized one route to the cafeteria was marked by a large mirror at the far end of the hall. Thereafter, he arrived at dinner by walking towards himself.

To travel to Greta's apartment, I turn left at the mandala rock, right at the bluebird house, and go straight to the ceramic dachshunds. She liked to cook, so I've been looking for a child-sized kitchen range to place outside her door.

Temple Grandin, an animal behaviorist, writes about three kinds of thinkers: visual, music and math, and verbal logic. She believes we assume everyone operates in the same area as ourselves. For example, I'm a verbal logic thinker and assume everyone loves words. Janell frequently (patiently) reminds me this isn't true. ("*Nobody cares about the logic behind bingo!*") My youngest son is a solid math thinker, and fought with high school teachers who insisted he write out, in English, the process he used to solve a math problem. ("*Math is a precise language. English is random. Why should I use an imperfect language to describe math?*")

As Greta ages, I see her move from verbal to visual thinking. She doesn't analyze her thinking, but I see the clues. She leaves the bingo room and turns down a hall. I know it's the wrong hallway (bingo is in the independent wing; Greta lives in the assisted wing) but I let her go. I know she will get partway down, realize her mistake, turn around and reappear in the central lobby.

"This looks like my hall," she told me. "My room is down and to the left."

"You're right," I say. "But this is the wrong hall. I know, they all look the same and I get confused too. Let's wander over this way instead."

Chasing after her to correct the mistake would point out the lapse in memory and humiliate and annoy her. Better to wait until she appears in the lobby, commiserate, then passively steer her to a known location.

Those of us working with a fully functional brain recognize and remember things like room numbers and hallway directions. That part of Greta is fading away. Honestly, I think numbers and names are boring; I would find it much more appealing to navigate via whimsical visuals.

What will Janell think when I hang a moose head in the kitchen and tell her it's a navigational aid?

Hallway Artwork

Walking to Greta's apartment, I noticed the artwork on the walls.

It's bland: something you see in hotel lobbies. Let us ponder the classic painting of the genre, titled "Hunting Grouse." It's a wash of fall colors, mostly orange fading to brown. There is, predictably, a grouse in flight and a hunter in the distant background. The bird is flying to the left, the hunter is walking to the right. The subjects of the painting are trying their hardest to escape this mundane print.

This art is designed to be less interesting the longer you look at it. These paintings are chosen so the colors of the art match the paint of the hallway, rather than choosing wall colors to accentuate the art. The corporate Optics and Design department strives for a calming theme that won't disrupt anyone's delicate sensibilities.

This pisses me off. Who the hell made the decision I need to be calmed? Some corporate focus group concluded if us members of this senior community are presented with visually challenging artwork we will require weeks of therapy. Worse, our children and heirs will initiate lawsuits to collect for mental anguish.

Corporate design teams forget I live with college professors. Poets. Musicians. Librarians. World War II veterans who RAN into combat with a single-shot carbine and a green cotton shirt. I live with men and women who crippled themselves on a potato field but now miss their farm. How dare they present a piece of art intended to calm. me. down. WTF?

I have discovered the current art is mounted with adhesive tape - not screws. With one quick yank, I could replace "Pheasant on the Prairie" with Dali's "The Persistence of Memory." I could dismount the western landscape and replace it with John Berkey's "Feather Ship."

Remember Dave Smith? He was the Scarabocchio guy and a former resident of Evergreen Meadows. Were he still alive, I would sneak to his door late at night (after 6:00 pm) and invite him to help me replace bad with good.

This artwork rebellion would require help. A resident at the far end of the building could push their pendant, summoning the late-night staff. It takes ten minutes to walk from the staff room to the far apartment, reset the pendant, then return. Dave and I would have five minutes to remove "Sunset Over The Desert" and hang "The Sly Shy Spotted Sagacious Snipper Snapper."

I estimate there are ten prints per hall. The memory wing doesn't have wall art, and the independent wing doesn't have staff (we assume we can do what we want with artwork in the independent wing, although that may not be true). That leaves three wings with about thirty prints Dave and I would have to clandestinely replace. This presents three problems: our artwork supply, willing accomplices, and movement of the artwork.

Thirty prints is a lot. This isn't stuff you find at Fleet Farm; you have to procure it. I'm guessing residents have favorite artwork stored with children and would agree to it hanging in our hallways. Janell and I have been entrusted with one such piece, "*Pumpkin and Table*." I'm sure Alberta, the former owner, would take delight in the wickedness of the entire project and approve the donation.

I'm certain we can enlist residents to distract the staff. The pendants are known to randomly trigger so the consequences of a button push are minimal. If we have a cadre of five button-pushers, we should be good to go.

Imagine our logistics-director-in-charge-of-art-replacement standing in front of the white board in the activity room. A floor plan of Evergreen Meadows Senior Community is sketched out in red dry-erase marker.

"Our target is Western Sunset with Cowboy hanging outside of the director's office," says our logistics director. She draws a green circle on the floor plan. "Bob, you'll move to the end of the independent wing, second floor, right near the elevator." A black circle indicates Bob's position.

"Margaret, you'll position strike team alpha in the first floor unisex bathroom. You will have the substitute Picasso '*The Three Musicians*'."

"I don't like the unisex bathroom," says Margaret. "It doesn't get cleaned often enough. Can we use the women's bathroom instead?"

"The women's bathroom is thirty feet away from the target," says our logistics director. "The unisex bathroom is right across the hall. Given that everyone in the strike team is using walkers, the distance is critical. Use the unisex bathroom, you'll need the extra time."

"Zeta Team," she continues, "you will be in the auditorium for the late-night movie. At precisely 8:00 p.m., Bob will trigger his pendant and you discretely leave the movie and move towards Alpha team." The logistics director draws a black box with arrows pointing in the direction of movement. "Don't mess this up again. The movie is supposed to be Titanic. If you don't want to miss the conclusion, watch it beforehand."

"Zeta team will pass the staff heading towards Bob. When Zeta team reaches the target, they will remove Western Sunset with Cowboy and proceed to room 423, which is the designated drop zone. Leave the print under the bed. Return to your rooms via different routes. When you pass the unisex bathroom, knock three times." Logistics demonstrates this knock on the table top. "Alpha team, that is your signal to hang your substitute."

"Remember, you can't be quick, so be efficient," she caps her dry-erase marker. "Any questions?"

There is the issue of moving thirty new prints into the building and moving the replaced artwork out. Administration or staff are going to take note of the arrivals, even if spaced out over time. Taking the old prints to the dumpster is sure to be noticed, especially since transporting a large print on a walker would be a dead giveaway of the nefarious plot.

I won't disclose how this would be accomplished. But if I were trying to curtail this project, I would be suspicious of sons or daughters with a pick-up truck and a tarp. Maybe that Sunday afternoon visit isn't just taking grandpa out for lunch…

The Beauty We Miss

For art to be appreciated, you must spend time with it. Flipping through a coffee-table book about the Louvre will not reveal the wonder of the Mona

Lisa. You must spend time looking at her eyes. You must see the delicate veil over her hair. Who else was in the studio? Why is she smiling?

To appreciate the community I live with takes time. You can't wander through on a Sunday afternoon and hope to notice subtle details. You will walk by the artwork of the grouse and hunter but never see it. You'll never look up and notice the umbrella at the corner of California and Florida. If your parent bothers to explain this umbrella, you might dismiss the whole story as another symptom of an aging mind.

You can't just march in and expect the world to reveal itself at your demand. Instead, you must be patient and allow the hallway to unfold as it is ready. There are comfortable chairs—you should try one.

Later, when you depart, would you do me a favor? If you see any artwork around the rear of the building, please discretely place it in the back of your pickup. You may keep it or dispose of it as you see fit. Strike Team Zeta appreciates your assistance.

Ruby

Ruby's legs are short and she has some trouble walking, but manages to get where she wants to go and get there when she wants to be there. You might wish for more rapid progress towards a destination, but that's something you want—not Ruby.

Ruby frequently visits Evergreen Meadows Senior Community. Her many friends know when to expect her visit and gather together in one place so as not to inconvenience her. They chat and socialize. Ruby doesn't understand the conversation, but is attentive and interested. What more could you want from a good friend?

Greta has never been friendly with Ruby's ilk. Greta tolerates her visits, but doesn't really want her around. Ruby senses this stand-offishness and works extra hard to win Greta's favor. I've never seen much progress, but Ruby does her best.

Ruby has large brown eyes framed by her brown hair. Her facial features are arranged loosely around her head. Her nose and ears are located where they are supposed to be, but not in a way that we think represent timeless beauty. She does not wear earrings but never leaves the house without a necklace.

She wears a thick coat. The same coat, both winter and summer. It would seem to be too warm on some days during the summer, but she wears it anyways. I doubt she considers taking it off.

Ruby never fails to make a stop by memory care. Some of her friends have recently moved there and she likes to touch base with them. She checks their room to see if they are sleeping, then wanders down to the central area. Like a good conversationalist, she wanders from resident to resident, inquiring about their health and providing comfort.

Visits only last so long until Ruby gets tired and needs a nap. She gets a ride back home and retires to the couch. The TV may be displaying a game show, but she doesn't much care about all the yelling and excitement.

In her dreams, Ruby chases birds. She wags her tail and thinks about dinner.

Angels Among Us

As part of our efforts to improve Greta's strength, Janell and I have been taking Greta on strolls. She slouches over her walker.

"Walk like a super model," Janell tells her. "Tits Up!"

Greta and Janell laugh; I try to maintain a sense of proper son-in-law decorum. Greta straightens her back, and we resume our walk.

Eloping

When we first arrived, Greta was in hospice and could not get out of bed without prodding. She has remarkedly improved to walking around the parking lot. Buoyed by success, I decided to enlarge our territory. Greta and I walk to the end of the sidewalk and instead of turning left at the property boundaries, we turn right towards the garden center on the next block. It's an ambitious goal, but I'm confident she will make it. If not, she can sit on her walker and I can push her home.

She struggles with the distance, but makes it. We are rewarded with a stroll through the nursery, and she mentions some of the vegetables she'd like to plant this next year. I conveniently neglect to remind her she no longer has a garden.

This all seems like a great achievement until I am called into the ~~principal's~~ administration office the next day.

"Mark," the administrator of Evergreen Meadows Senior Community says. "We saw you walking Greta around the block yesterday."

"I know," I say, filled with pride. "By next week we can be walking to the shopping mall!"

"That is a problem," she says. "You are helping Greta become used to traveling off the property. She may wander off and forget how to get home. If she returns to Evergreen Meadows in the back seat of a police car, we have to either place her in memory care or she has to find a new place to live. And right now, we don't have any room in memory care."

Again I am being told to *straighten up, buster*. Nicely, but the message is clear.

When residents wander off-property, this is called "eloping." It is different from the high-school ill-advised marriage activity. But like marriage eloping, participants sometimes get lost and sometimes get in trouble. Families become upset and take legal action. That's bad. I shouldn't be teaching Greta to wander.

Late Nights

Greta has been pacing the halls of Evergreen Meadows Senior Community. Normally not a problem—I lurk around the halls as well. The difference between Greta and me is that Greta shouts "HELP. WHERE IS EVERYBODY?" The staff helps her get back to her room and safely back in bed.

Yesterday the staff saw her heading out of the parking lot. They send Joan to chase her down.

"Greta," says Joan. "Where are you going?"

"I'm heading to the cafeteria," she responds without stopping. "I'm late for lunch."

It's actually dinner time, and she is heading for the highway. Both are clear indicators; it's time for Greta to move to the memory care unit.

The decision to move Greta is difficult. Greta is chatty and social. Most of the folks in memory care are neither. Worse, Greta knows what memory care is all about. She's been back there to visit some friends and was able to carry on one-way conversations. She was relieved to make it back out of the locked doors keeping residents from wandering into the street. But this is inescapable; Greta needs the extra support she will receive from the memory care staff.

Her children concoct an elaborate plot to move her into this new apartment. Some of us take her out for the weekend. Others take advantage of her absence to carry things to the new place and store things she won't need or that won't fit. On Sunday evening, we return with Greta.

Instead of turning right, we go straight into the memory care wing.

"Where are we going?" Greta says. She points to the right. "My apartment is that way."

"Mom," Janell says, and heads towards the locked door. "Let's go look at your new apartment."

The memory wing is like my college dorm. It has a shared bathroom and opens into a central space. There is a large television and sitting area. There are always people to talk to. Even better, there is a patio for sunny afternoons, a 24-hour kitchen and personal staff.

Unlike my dorm, the door to the outside world is locked.

Greta is in transition. She isn't able to manage on her own and the staff in this wing provide the things she needs. But she is chatty. Much more so than her peers. She simultaneously doesn't know enough and also knows too much.

I join Greta at mealtimes and talk while she eats. During one of her first days, we have a discussion about "this place."

"Why am I here?" she asks me. "What test do I have to take to get out and back to my old apartment?"

"It's not a test," I tell her. "It's because part of your brain doesn't work. This place is like your walker. You use it since your legs don't work like they used to. This place, and the staff here, help you with the things you aren't able to do on your own. There are things your brain doesn't remember anymore."

"I don't need this," she says.

"Where are you living right now?" I ask her.

"I don't know," she admits.

"You are in Stevens Point," I tell her. "How is your lunch?"

"It's not good. The beans are dry," She pokes at the beans. If Ruby were nearby, she would clandestinely hand the beans to the dog. But she never allowed dogs in her house, so perhaps she never learned that trick. Or the kids never had a dog precisely because she knew that trick.

"How about the meat loaf?" I ask. She has eaten most of it already.

"It's not as good as mine," she laughs.

"Where are you living right now?" I ask her.

"I don't know," she admits. She doesn't remember I just told her the answer.

I'm trying to make a case for why she needs memory care; ironically, because she needs memory care, she can't fathom my logic. I change the topic.

In a few months, Greta will slip below the cognitive threshold where she is bothered by the lack of conversation with her peers. On the positive, she engages with more activities than when she was in assisted living. She gets more personal attention from the staff. When she gets up at night, there is always someone to reassure her that she isn't alone. They ask her if she would like a snack and a glass of juice. They listen to audio books with her.

Greta is surrounded by caring people. They like her and care for her with enthusiasm and sincerity. She calls me her favorite son-in-law, but I know she has many "favorite" people in her life.

My mother called them "angels among us." I am honored to be one of them.

Only Two Months

Janell and I have an open-ended lease of this apartment and could stay here as long as we wish. It's expensive, but comfortable and convenient. We've provided 24x7 physical therapy for Greta and make an enormous difference in her quality of life. It's a tempting place to spend a year.

But we have a life in Portland. We have friends, an ocean, a house, a neighborhood. Our neighbor dog sticks his head through a hole in the fence and whines for biscuits. Our chickens lay eggs. We belong to clubs and a church. All of that is on hold until we return. We can't do it online.

We've explained this to Greta, but we know her weakening grasp of *now* versus *then* versus *tomorrow* blurs her awareness of the pending change in her life. She is accustomed to us appearing before breakfast to wake her up, then seeing her through the day until it is time for bed. Today is the last day this will happen.

I'm watching Zero chase the local squirrel for the last time this summer, possibly this year, possibly forever, depending on Tom and Pauline (Tom and Pauline own Zero). Everything we bought from Goodwill has been returned.

One of our last acts is saying goodbye to our friends. This takes too long, but should go on forever. We lurk through the building, saying hello and goodbye. But oh, that final walk through the dining hall is hard.

I exchange last jokes and stories and move from table to table. I look into Margaret's eyes. I swap quips with the ladies of table number one. But the best moment is when Charles walks by.

Charles watches too much opinion television and likes to discuss the latest conspiracies. He wears a baseball cap. I first met Charles when he called me over at lunch one day early in our stay;

"Hey, are you from Portland?" Charles shouted.

I wasn't sure where this would lead, but I responded positively.

"What are you doing about all those homeless people?" he asked. At the time, this was a hot topic for opinion television. The TV discussion was peppered with the terms "trash," "criminals", and "drug addicts." The newscast displayed streets with rows of tents, disheveled men, and piles of dismembered bicycles.

"That's a tough question," I responded. "We're trying to figure out how best to help all the children stuck in poverty and veterans with PTSD from their war experiences."

Charles stopped mid-response. His hat displays the name of his battleship during the Korean war. He may have realized some of those homeless drug addicts on the TV are his brothers-in-arms.

From that moment on, we explored stories with our different viewpoints. We always part with a laugh and agree it's up to us. Charles is a hard-won, and most valued friend.

Charles uses a walker, and deviations from a direct path are an extra effort for him. Today, he gets up from his table in the corner and begins the walk back to his room. This time he drifts to the right, away from the exit, towards where I'm sitting with Margaret.

"I hear you're leaving," Charles says.

"Yep," I agree. "Leaving in about an hour."

"Well… I'm going to miss you." That's it. He heads towards the exit. But what more does he need to say? It's a sonnet in six words.

This is the last time I will see some of these friends, but I don't know whom. Some of the most sickly will be here when we visit again. Some of our healthy friends will not.

When my parents were still alive, I was sitting in their living room, talking with them about the extensive collection of art, furniture, books, and souvenirs in their house. When it came time to move them to assisted living, it would be my task to move all of their stuff. I encouraged them to give it to charities or Goodwill.

"You should take the things you want," said my mother. I lived in the other corner of the country, three thousand miles away. Hauling keepsakes across that distance was impractical. Besides, I had a house full of my own possessions.

"Thanks, but that's just not possible," I said.

"Don't worry," my dad responded to my mom. "When you die, I'll just back up a dumpster and throw everything away."

My father never hit my mother or abused her in any way. But this time, I don't know why he didn't just reach over and slap her. From her expression, his comments were just as painful.

My father was tossing out more than art and furniture. My mother had carefully bestowed meaning onto each item. Like an urn filled with the cremated ashes of a beloved relative, each dish and each chair contained the echo of a precious person, place, or thing. We could point to any item and she would relate the story of a picnic with a special friend, or the time she went to visit her favorite aunt's house and had a special cookie with tea.

Throwing out the broken rocking chair would end the physical existence of Grandma Dietze. The painting of *Christina's World* hung above the dry sink was the last gift from a now-deceased friend. The tin pie cabinet was rescued from her mother-in-law's back porch in Cook, Nebraska before the family house was sold. These objects were the last evidence any of this had happened.

For us, today, leaving was the equivalent of backing a dumpster up to the front door of Evergreen Meadows Senior Community. All the marbles, figurines, medallions, agates, walkers, and jewelry that remind me of the residents would be at risk. Every day, one of those trinkets might disappear, along with the memory of that resident.

I don't know if Charles's baseball cap will go missing. I don't know if he will be here when I get back. It makes leaving here all the more difficult. I've unwittingly made a second life and I can't have both this life in Stevens Point, Wisconsin and my other life in Portland, Oregon.

Janell and I say (another) final goodbye to Greta in her room, then walk towards the front door. It's not a linear path, but is affected by the gravity of friends sitting in the front hall, heading to lunch, or on their way to bingo. It takes a well-spent hour to move across the lobby. Outside, we chat with the ladies watching the parking lot, another fifteen minutes. It's as if we have nowhere else to be. Certainly no where else more important. Our car is just over there, full of travel gear and ready for the five-day drive to the Pacific Coast. We sit in the front seat of our car, take a deep breath and turn the key. The engine starts and we turn to the west.

Coda

I wake up at two o'clock in the morning. The tree outside our Portland house bends the streetlight into fractal patterns. If I open my eyes, I'll admit I'm awake and can't go back to sleep. Janell is ~~gently~~ snoring next to me, which she'll do for another half-hour before she returns to deep sleep. I get up and leave her to her dreams.

I know it's two in the morning because I heard my father's clock chiming the hour. It's a Seth-Thomas Ogee, built between 1842 and 1913. It has two weights; one for the clock and one for the chime, and it rings out each hour. No fancy Westminster chimes; just once for one-o'clock, two for two-o'clock. The clockworks are in plain sight when I open the glass front to wind it up.

I also received a clock from my mother. It is much more ornate and the chime is louder and more melodious. Its clockworks are hidden inside the case and when it rings the hour, it is much more demanding of attention and keeps everyone awake. We don't wind the alarm anymore but I can hear it tick-tock all the way downstairs. In my teenage years, my mother waited up for me to come home from a night of youthful disobedience; her clock has the same late-night presence.

I go to the kitchen for a snack. I keep a jar of pickled Spicy Brussels sprouts for this sort of thing. Janell hates them, so I enjoy the treat without feeling the need to save some for her.

I pour a glass of water and head back to the stairs, passing the living room. I hear someone humming. I glance over, and see Greta sitting in the red chair. Both she and the chair seem to be content.

My rational self knows Greta is 1,945 miles to the east, sleeping in her bed at Evergreen Meadows Senior Community. She isn't here, just as the red chair doesn't manifest ghosts.

"Hello Marky," she says. "What are you doing up so late?"

I sit on the couch and place my water on the side table. “Couldn’t sleep,” I say. “What are you doing here?”

“There’s lots of places I can be. I don’t have to choose. So I’m here.”

“But you’re in Stevens Point.”

“Some of me is. Some of me isn’t. The parts of me you don’t see in Stevens Point don’t cease to exist, they just fade from one place and show up somewhere else.”

I try to remember our conversations in her home where I first met her. She loved to play cribbage, so like a good host, I get a deck of cards and a cribbage board.

“Cribbage?” I ask. I pull up a small table, put out the board and deal the cards.

“I thought you didn’t play cribbage?” she asks.

“You taught me. I play on special occasions.”

“I’d love to,” Greta responds. “But you’re going to have to help me with cards. My hands don’t hold things very well. I guess that’s one of the things still in Stevens Point.”

I’m not very good at cribbage, but Greta is patient. She used to always win, but when I’ve played with her in Stevens Point, she has a hard time remembering how the game is scored. I can be equally patient.

I spread the cards out and Greta points at one of them. I turn it over; a four of hearts. I draw an ace of diamonds, so I get the first crib. I deal six cards to each of us and put two cards in my crib. Greta points at two cards and I place them in the crib as well. Greta points at a card in her hand on the table; I turn it over. It’s a nine of clubs.

I play a two of spades. She plays a three of hearts. I play an ace. For that, I get 2 points for fifteen, three points for a run. I’m feeling cocky until Greta plays a second ace for two points. We play out the cards, count out the pairs, I count crib. She plays confidently, I sputter along, trying not to make a mistake. The round ends with Greta at 10 points, I’m at fourteen.

“What’s it like?” I ask. I deal for Greta, cut the deck.

"What's what like?" She points to cards and tells me to add them to her crib.

"Death. Heaven. The afterlife?" I play the four of hearts.

"I don't know," says Greta. "Ask me after I'm dead. But even then I won't be able to tell you much." She plays the four of diamonds for two points.

"Because you signed an NDA?" I play the four of spades for six points.

"No," Greta laughs. "Because these spoken words don't have what it takes to describe it. Explaining it is kind of like talking to chickens, right? We'll be happier if we don't try to puzzle it out."

The round ends with Greta at twenty-eight, me at twenty-three. I pause, take a drink of water, shuffle and deal. What do you ask a ghost, or whatever it is I am talking to? How to get rich? How to be all-powerful? Where did I misplace my keys?

"You told me once you thought about becoming a nun." Greta plays an eight of clubs, I play seven of hearts for two points.

Greta plays the seven of clubs for two points. "I did," she says.

I play six of hearts. "What stopped you?"

"I met Eugene," says Greta. "Go."

I play the ace of clubs. "You decided you'd rather hang out with Gene?"

Greta repeats "Go," I play the six of clubs. Greta plays the jack of diamonds.

"He was gone a lot. He was in Chicago working for the railroad. Ask him. Mom and Dad knew who he was."

I play eight of hearts. "What did your mom and dad think of him?"

Greta gets sixteen points from her count. "Gene knew his dad ran around. He wasn't going to live a life like that."

I get ten points from cards and crib. I gather the cards and deal. It's Greta's crib, I give her an eight of clubs and queen of diamonds.

I lead with a two of spades and ask another question about Gene. "Was Gene a good dancer?"

"No," says Greta. She plays the eight of diamonds. "He had two left feet. But he tried. But he knew I liked to dance. And he liked music. But not to dance. If he was having fun, that's all I cared."

"You'll get to see Gene again, right?" I put down the five of clubs for two points.

"Because if anyone is in heaven, he's in heaven." Greta plays a seven of clubs. I play the two of diamonds, she plays the seven of hearts for a count of 31 and two more points.

I play the five of spades. "Yeah—I think you two will play cards."

"In heaven?" Greta asks? She plays the eight of hearts for one point. "Well, they better play for nickels. Gene wins a lot."

We count. I get eight points. Greta gets 24 plus one point from the crib. The score is Greta 75 to my 48.

I deal, cut, and put cards in the crib. Greta plays the nine of hearts. "Do you think you'll see your mom again?" I ask. I return a six of diamonds.

Greta plays the ten of spades. "I'll see her in heaven."

"What will that be like?" I play the ace of clubs. She says go, and I play the ace of spades for two points.

"I don't know," she replies. Her tone is somewhere between puzzled and annoyed. I have to admit, it was a dumb question. Greta's not dead; how would she know?

She's up to eighty-eight points to my fifty-seven. Greta still has her cribbage chops.

"What do you want to be remembered for?" I ask. "When I tell grandchildren about you, what should i tell them?"

Greta looks up from cards. "I loved life," she says. "There's a lot of things in life you embrace that you don't care for, but the majority is good. So look for the good sides. Kindness should be your aim."

"Is Janell coming down?" she asks.

"I doubt it. I'll tell her you were here."

"Don't bother. I'll tell her myself." Greta is fading from view. "Tell her she made a good choice when she married you."

I look up and she is gone. Just an empty red chair, a cribbage board, and a glass of water. The house is quiet except for the clock.

I'm planning to live to be a hundred: not an exaggeration. When Greta isn't able to laugh at my jokes, I'll need to find someone else to carry on that task. I guess that's one reason (among many) to delight in grandchildren.

I'm a better person because of the time I have spent with Greta. I look forward to spending more time with her peers—who will quickly become my peers. I've decided to embrace my age with enthusiasm and try to live up to the lessons I've learned from my favorite mother-in-law.

Acknowledgments

The Ross family has always been gracious and welcoming, traits they learned from Greta. I am grateful for their memories and permission to document my experiences. Thanks, Bob, Kathleen, and Connie.

I am part of the exclusive club of Ross in-laws. We joke and snark about the siblings, but we love them dearly. Thanks Lisa and Mike. We're going to write a handbook on surviving with the Ross family. And Mike; let me know when it is your turn to be the favorite son-in-law. I'll be happy to ship you the T-shirt, ballcap, and lapel pin.

The barn and repository for stolen property was courtesy of Jon and Sharon (and Iris, Ike, and Ruby). Thanks for not kicking me out of the dorm room, even when I deserved it.

I am grateful to the assisted living facility where much of this happened. They requested I respect the anonymity of staff and residents, but you know who you are and hopefully, you know the universe of respect I have for you and your profession. Thank you for being Greta's best friends.

Ask any writer about the task of getting useful reviews and edits. Their response will start with an exasperated sigh, then you will hear of the difficulty of finding someone who will provide a useful review. I am indebted to Don Barnes, Robin Rolfe, Abbie Weisenbloom., John Goff, Janet Patin, Dick Morgan, Mari Partenheimer, Greg Moore, Paul Bigler, Amy Houchen, and Linda MacIntyre.

Finally, Janell. Thank you for welcoming me into your life and for the opportunity to meet one of the finest people I have ever known. I'm sorry I shrunk your laundry.

About The Author

Thank you for reading "My Favorite Mother-In-Law." If you enjoyed it, won't you please take a moment to leave me a review at your favorite retailer?

Mark Niemann-Ross writes mostly science fiction, sometimes programming in R, often about tinkering with Raspberry Pi (the single board computer, not the pastry).

He lives in Portland, Oregon, paddles boats, and gives compliments to strangers.

You can find him at http://www.niemannross.com, LinkedIn, GitHub, Goodreads, and Mastodon.

Other Titles by Mark Niemann-Ross

Stupid Machine: Car accidents don't happen in 2060. Which makes Jordan Bishop's fatal crash in a self-driving vehicle unusual. Maybe even a murder. But who can tell? *Science Fiction*

Humanity by Proxy: Humanity by Proxy and Other Stories celebrates the positive aspects of technology and it's designers. *Science Fiction*

Patches Catches the Sargo County Cattle Rustler: Patches, a talented Border Collie, teams up with his young owner to outwit a cattle rustler in the old west. John is left in charge of his younger sister when his parents are called away on an emergency. When he finds a desperate outlaw in the kitchen, his only defense is a good story – and Patches. *Juvenile*

Learn More about My Favorite Mother-In-Law

There's a lot happening in the world of this book. Find out more at this website:

More about my Favorite Mother-In-Law

www.ingramcontent.com/pod-product-compliance
Ingram Content Group UK Ltd.
Pitfield, Milton Keynes, MK11 3LW, UK
UKHW062312290726
14090UKWH00018B/1017